Stephen L Priest

May 15, 2016

Enjoy!
Steve

Outdoor Play
"Fun 4 4 Seasons"
Volume II

By

Stephen L. Priest

OutdoorSteve.com

Also by Stephen L. Priest

- *Outdoor Play "Fun 4 4 Seasons" Volume I*
  978-0-985-03840-3

- *Outdoor Enthusiast: Never Say, "I Wish I Had ..."*
  ISBN - 1440438404

- *Avoiding Injuries: Tips from Master Outdoorsman Steve Priest*
  ISBN 9781440438455

- *Outdoor Enthusiast: Never Say, "I wish I had ..." e-book*
  ISBN – 13: 9780615225050

Cover Design by LoonsNest.biz

Outdoor Play
"Fun 4 4 Seasons"
Volume II

© 2017 by Stephen L. Priest

www.outdoorsteve.com

ISBN-10: 0-9850384-2-X
ISBN-13: 978-0-9850384-2-7

Preface

Outdoor Play "Fun 4 4 Seasons" Volume II

By

Stephen L. Priest

Steve's mission is to motivate and encourage families and individuals to make the outdoors a key component of their daily life. **Outdoor Play "Fun 4 4 Seasons" Volume II** continues the insights and healthy lifestyle of outdoor activities of **Outdoor Play "Fun 4 4 Seasons" Volume I**. Steve's stories and lessons make you want to put on your backpack, find your running shoes, borrow a canoe from the neighbor, tune-up the bike, and get ready for cross country skiing!

Some folks call outdoor experiences 'play'. If play is defined as the choice made to take a course of action based on the rewards of participation, and getting a perspective that can only come from 'doing', then indeed outdoor adventures are play. In fact, many adults and children do not play enough.

Outdoor exercise has proven to make you healthier both physically and mentally. Your mind gets relieved of personal and business stress and the result is a positive outlook on life. Your body gets stronger with outdoor movement and presence and the breathing of fresh air. All this helps to avoid injuries.

We began by looking in our own backyard where we saw animals, flora, rivers and ponds – and then within a few hours of our homes. Paddling amongst the foliage of October in northern New England, all I could think of was a Michelangelo painting. We visited the coast of Maine, and then we were off paddling among its coastal islands. The boundary waters of Minnesota and Ontario summoned us. The Grand Canyon gave us beauty beyond verbal description.

With each outing, I brought my camera, and when the time came to select pictures for the book, the memories they conveyed made it difficult to limit myself to only a few.

The beginning of **Outdoor Play "Fun 4 4 Seasons Volume II** offers a process to be an outdoor enthusiast for those who hesitate because of age, limited time, family commitments, or knowledge of an activity.

The middle sections are divided into the seasons of the year, **Spring, Summer, Fall** and **Winter** with glimpses of Steve's own outdoor undertakings. These sections are taken from the last three years of Steve's blog – **Outdoor Adventurers**. Steve provides a peek into outdoor places and Internet sites to assist you in your research and preparation.

The next to last section, **Places to Play in Northern New England**, provides web references to local activities and clubs to join as incentives to learn and participate – if indeed you need these supports.

The last section, **The Beginning**, is Steve's own personal story of how he went from a couch potato to a daily outdoor enthusiast.

"Everyone must believe in something. I believe I'll go canoeing." - Henry David Thoreau

Dedication

Linwood "The Loon" Parsons
Betty "The Chickadee" Parsons

For sharing your outdoor wisdom
A lifetime of special memories
Plus
3 Allagash Canoe Expeditions!

Acknowledgements

My wife Cathy has been steadfast in her encouragement of my daily outdoor commitment. Amongst many of our outdoor activities, Cathy and I have swam, hiked, camped, paddled, walked, and run together. She has been my support team throughout my life.

My sons Tim and Shaun, and friends John Kerrigan, Dundee Nestler, Paul Nestler, and Michael Dionian have been my consistent outdoor enthusiast partners. Shaun, Tim, Sandra Priest, and my cousin Linwood Parsons have been my confidants and proofreaders throughout the preparation of this book.

Jefferson Nunn was bold enough to see visions of sharing my stories with other outdoor enthusiasts, as well as those wanting to be. His underlying support for my books as well as my web site (**OutdoorSteve.com**) has been very much appreciated.

Linwood Parsons' deep collaboration with me from start to finish of this book, and for his computer design talents in creating the graphic design for the cover, graphics, and pictures, is beyond a simple "thanks".

My outdoor enthusiast friends encouraged me to go to the woods, lakes, and rivers of northern New Hampshire, and before we realized it, we had regular outdoor excursions. My cousin Linwood took us to the Allagash Wilderness Waterway in Maine – three times in fact! Other friends heard our wilderness stories and read my Outdoor Enthusiast blog, and then, all of a sudden, we had yearly outdoor commitments.

I thank George Potter for encouraging me to start my Outdoor Enthusiast Blog http://outdooradventurers.blogspot.com/. This blog has provided most of the material in **Outdoor Play 4 4 Seasons Volume I** and **Outdoor Play 4 4 Seasons Volume II.**

My earlier books were arranged by chapters of outdoor activities (e.g. running, hiking, canoeing, skiing, triathlons) – whereas the **Outdoor Play Fun 4 4 Seasons Volume I** and **II** series are arranged by the seasons of the activities presented (e.g. **Spring, Summer, Fall** and **Winter**).

My Dad had a great love of Maine, and my Mom saw that we - seven children and all the grandchildren - were encouraged in our outdoor endeavors. One of my favorite memories of Mom was hearing the race timer in my first race tell me Mom would not let him leave until I had crossed the finish line - in last place and all by myself!

My granddaughter, Madison, was my support team in one of my triathlons, a companion hiker up Mt Washington, and a Green River Reservoir flint and steel fire lighter. My grandson Carson is featured in both the canoe rescue training in the **Summer** section and has his own Warrior dash competition section where his grandparents served as his support team. As a family we hike, swim, paddle, and enjoy sports in all seasons.

The book you are about to read is not about me. I certainly may be the central character in the stories, but in addition to the aforementioned, Dick Satter, Tom Austin, Lennie Carroll, Joe Ryan, Ron Millett, Linda Nestler, Betty Parsons, Austin Priest, Braden Priest, David Priest, Dennis Priest, Helen Priest, Leanne Priest, and Marlene Priest have all been part of my outdoor life.

Bedford Community Television (BCTV) – (http://www.bedfordtv.com/) has generously shown many of my documentaries on their TV station.

For those friends I have inadvertently left out, 'thank you.'

Contents

How to Become an Outdoor Enthusiast

"Everyone must believe in something. I believe I'll go outdoors." – S. Priest

Outdoor Play "Fun 4 4 Seasons" Volume II enthusiastically portrays a daily commitment to the outdoors for health and fitness. This book is full of personal "how does it feel" insights and references for the reader to learn more.

The message is to get outdoors and do something. Often your quest starts in your own neighborhood and community. Do not worry about reaching the top of the mountain - just concern yourself with staying on the path. The only competition you have is the task at hand.

Exercise has proven to make you healthier both physically and mentally. Making a commitment to daily outdoor activities, such as walking and running, add to your endurance for all outdoor activities. Best yet, your body will be stronger with exercise, thus avoiding many injuries. So how do you get started being an outdoor enthusiast?

Some people can be discouraged from exercising by not knowing what to do or how to do it. Those who were athletic in childhood may be frustrated by how their abilities have deteriorated over time. Certain individuals need to try new activities so they won't be comparing themselves to others or earlier performances.

This first section is an introduction to the major intent of this book - to promote the outdoors as a component of one's daily life. I will suggest a process to become an outdoor enthusiast for those who hesitate because of age, limited time, family commitments, or knowledge of an activity. I have used this process to get where I am today.

The middle sections are divided into the seasons of the year: **Spring**, **Summer**, **Fall** and **Winter** with glimpses into my own outdoor feelings and shared learning with supporting web references and videos. These sections are taken from the last four years of my blog – **Outdoor Enthusiast**. These posts provide a peek into outdoor places and Internet sites for additional research and preparation.

The **Places to Play in Northern New England** section provides web references to local activities and clubs to join as incentives to learn and participate.

The last section, **The Beginning**, is my personal story of how I went from a couch potato with a limp from a torn Achilles tendon injury to a daily outdoor enthusiast.

You are only limited to an outdoor activity by boundaries set by yourself. Just by following simple steps, you will be well on your way to expanding your horizons and removing barriers and boundaries to enjoying the outdoors and a healthier you.

In my case I will start the "beginner" reader with walking outdoors or on a treadmill. Progression to outside exercise is presented as distances between telephone poles. I will explain "telephone poles" later.

First, like all advice on exercise, it is strongly recommended you get your physician's approval.

Second, it is OK for a family member or friend to join you in this endeavor, BUT DO NOT WAIT because of their schedule. Rely on no one but yourself. No excuses.

No matter which outdoor exercises you choose, you need to get your cardio system in shape. Your heart is the engine that needs preparation and tuning. You can do this with both exercise and proper eating habits.

Frankly, in my case, the key is exercise and the eating habits will follow naturally. The more exercise I did, the better my eating awareness and habits became. This chapter does not focus on food. It addresses exercise, and in particular talks about gradually working up from simple and short walks, and the intensity and duration of the exercises will be determined over time.

Start Right Outside Your Home

What is great is you can start right outside your home! For safety's sake, remember to ALWAYS walk and run on the sidewalk, or on the side of the road facing oncoming traffic.

Keeping a diary of each day's progression, including how far you went, the method of exercise (walk, run/walk, run) will help motivate you when you see the progress you are making.

Next, RESIST TEMPTATION TO GO FASTER AND FURTHER. If you do, you will most assuredly be injured.

Okay, let's get started.

> **Day 1**: Go outside and walk the distance between two telephone poles, then walk back home.
> **Day 2**: Go outside and walk the distance between three telephone poles, then walk back home.
> **Day 3**: Go outside and walk the distance between four telephone poles, then walk back home.
>
> Continue this progressive program for days 4 and 5. If you have breathing problems, or get exhausted, do not add the extra distance.
>
> **Day 6 and 7**: Rest. Skip only two days a week. Light rain is no excuse for not accomplishing your day's goal.
> **Day 8**: Go outside and run the distance between two telephone poles, then walk back home.
> **Day 9**: Go outside and run the distance between four telephone poles, then walk back home.
> **Day 10, 11, 12**: Run six, eight and ten telephone poles respectively (yes, you have increased the number of poles).

If you have followed this fixed schedule, you will feel the urge to get into your car and measure your distance. Do it!
Now develop your own plan to reach one mile in six weeks.

Some frequently asked questions on getting started:

- How far is the distance between two telephone poles? ANSWER: Well, I have 60 paces (about 60 yards) between the poles on my street. No telephone poles? ANSWER: I just gave you a distance.

- What if I feel good and want to go further and faster? ANSWER: DO NOT, I repeat, DO NOT try walking or running beyond the specified distances. People, feeling good, try to go further and faster. THEY GET INJURED, and then they are set back for months. DO NOT, I repeat, DO NOT try to get ahead of this schedule.

- What if I am injured, such as with shin splints or a sore knee? ANSWER: Then back off a bit from your running distance and do more walking. As your injury pain subsides, return to an increased schedule. Try not to skip a daily run or walk, unless you feel the pain is causing the injury to worsen.

- Do I need a particular shoe or sneaker to start? ANSWER: Nope - no excuses. Get outside. When you reach day twelve, you are now ready to buy sneakers or running shoes.

- Do I need sweat pants, shorts, or polypropylene clothing? ANSWER: Nope, again no excuses. Get outside. When you reach day twelve, you are now ready to look like a runner – buy yourself some running shorts, light jacket and long lightweight pants.

- Do I need a hat? ANSWER: Yes. Old, new, torn or whatever. You need a hat to protect you from the sun and rain. Get outside.

Four reminders to becoming an outdoor enthusiast:

1. Be sure to follow the schedule of this program.

2. RESIST TEMPTATIONS TO GO FASTER AND FURTHER, or else, guaranteed, YOU WILL GET INJURED.

3. Be consistent in doing your walking and running. NO excuse to missing a day.

4. Do not let weather, lack of an outdoor companion, or fancy clothing deter you.

To get a sense of how another person did with this program, it took Outdoor Steve six weeks before he ran one mile without stopping to walk. Thereafter, he never exceeded one mile for the next year. After a year, he began to increase his distance. As he gained confidence in his physical conditioning, he complemented his running with other outdoor challenges. His accomplishments have included cycling, hiking, swimming, canoeing, kayaking, triathlons, biathlons, cross-country skiing, and marathons.

When presented with an outdoor opportunity, such as a one-week paddle on the one-hundred and seven-mile Allagash Wilderness Waterway, do I say, "I have too many things to do?" Or do I say, "Yes!" because this is a great opportunity to enjoy my sons and friends? The work and home chores will be there when I get back.

As you read the short stories in this book, let your body and mind experience the wonderment of personal enlightenment and outdoor play.

Most of these short scenarios are taken from my **Outdoor Enthusiast** blog (http://outdooradventurers.blogspot.com/). Each post has Internet references "what, where, why and how" so the reader can do much more than simply learn about one person's outdoor quests. These stories are intended to both motivate and instruct the reader by providing outdoor places to go and things to do.

My mission is to motivate and encourage families and individuals to make the outdoors a key component of their daily life.

Get on your bike. Go hiking with your family. Run with a neighbor. Take telemark ski lessons. Try an Ottertail paddle. Take swimming lessons. Go spinning on your bike. Visit a museum. Go to an Audubon seminar.

Never say, "I wish I had gone outdoors with family and friends".

Spring

Two roads diverged in a wood and I – I took the one less traveled by, and that has made all the difference – Robert Frost

A Barred Owl in New Hampshire

Figure 1 - Barred Owl

A large bird caught my eye as it landed on a tree branch in my winter wooded snowbound backyard. I immediately recognized the bird's unique owl look and brown-and-white-striped plumage. It was a **barred owl**. They can often reach 20 inches in height and have a wingspan of 43 inches.

Figure 2 - "Who cooks for you? Who cooks for you all?"

You will hear the barred owl's hooting call. The experts say it sounds like *"Who cooks for you? Who cooks for you-all?"* Me, well as you will hear it was not my imitation that attracted this owl. I have indeed heard its hoot call many times.

Fortunately my camera was nearby and you will get to enjoy this one minute video.

Notice in one picture the left eye is wide open, while the right eye is somewhat closed. Amazingly, many birds can essentially sleep with half of their brains - they keep one eye open and one side of their brain awake while the other side rests. That may be what's happening here - the owl may be going to sleep (or just

8

awakening) with its right eye and thus left brain. Interestingly, I have outdoor enthusiast friends who also sleep like that!

Try and see if you can imitate the barred owl's hooting call, "*Who cooks for you? Who cooks for you-all?*"

References

- **Video Reference: A Barred Owl in New Hampshire**
  http://outdooradventurers.blogspot.com/2015/03/a-barred-owl-in-new-hampshire.html
- All About Birds
  http://www.allaboutbirds.org/guide/Barred_Owl/sounds
- Winter in New Hampshire is more than downhill skiing
  http://outdooradventurers.blogspot.com/2015/02/winter-in-new-hampshire-is-more-than.html

Hiking Mt Kearsarge in Central New Hampshire

Mount Kearsarge is a 2,937 foot mountain located in the towns of Wilmot and Warner, New Hampshire. Our ascent to the summit starts at the Winslow State Park parking lot at the northwest slope of Mt. Kearsarge.

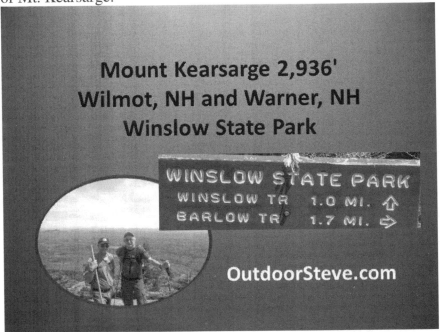

Figure 3 - Mount Kearsage, New Hampshire

Mount Kearsarge has multiple trails and a bare rockbound summit with an observation fire tower and a cell phone tower.

From the summit on a clear day lies a spectacular view of the White Mountains and Mt. Cardigan in the north, the Green Mountains and Mt. Sunapee in the west, and the Monadnock Region and the Merrimack Valley in the south. The summit with its towers is a distinctive landmark and is easily seen from its surrounding communities.

Figure 4 - The summit with its distinctive towers landmark

We chose to summit from Winslow State Park with the option of two trails. The Winslow Trail, marked with red blazes, begins at the park's parking area. Winslow Trail climbs for 1.1 miles (1,100 vertical feet) through the forest and over bare granite ledge to the 2,937-foot summit.

Figure 5 - Barlow or Winslow Trail?

The Barlow Trail, marked with yellow blazes, also leaves from the same parking area at Winslow Park and provides a longer, but more gradual ascent to the summit. Several vistas along the 1.7 mile trail afford views of the Andover area, Ragged Mountain, and Mount Cardigan.

We decided to ascend via the longer Barlow Trail and to descend using the much steeper but shorter Winslow Trail. The wet spring run-off and mossy rocks made today's Winslow Trail very slippery.

Early June is the black fly season, and they were plentiful on the day of our trek.

Enjoy this beautiful outdoor recreation of New Hampshire – never say, "I wish I had taken my family to climb Mt Kearsarge."

References

- **Video and Blog Post**- Hiking Mt Kearsage in Central New Hampshire
  http://outdooradventurers.blogspot.com/2014/06/hiking-mt-kearsarge-in-central-new.html

- Map and more information on Mt Kearsarge
  http://www.nhstateparks.org/uploads/pdf/KearsargeHiking Map_Web.pdf

Tuckerman Ravine, Southeast Face of Mt. Washington, White Mountains, New Hampshire

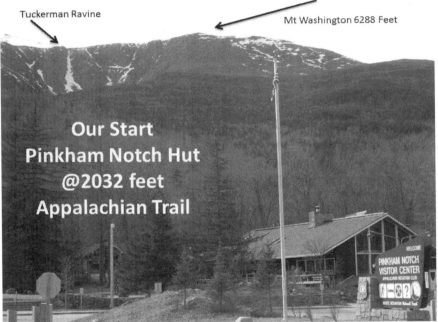

Tuckerman Ravine

Mt Washington 6288 Feet

Our Start
Pinkham Notch Hut
@2032 feet
Appalachian Trail

Figure 6 - View from Pinkham Notch AMC Hut

Tuckerman Ravine is one of New Hampshire's unique natural resources. My wife Catherine, friend Dundee, and I did an uphill 2.4 mile snow and ice packed hike to the base of Tuckerman. The short video below shares highlights from our 4 hour hike via the Tuckerman Ravine Trail. Our trek starts with the 2.5 hour hike from the Appalachian Mountain Club's Pinkham Notch Hut up to the Hermit Hut Shelter, and includes our 1.5 hour downhill hike return to our car.

Tuckerman Ravine is a vast open bowl perched on the southeast slope of Mount Washington, the highest mountain in the Northeast at 6,288 feet. In the spring, Ravine snow depths can reach 100 feet.

Figure 7 - Tuckerman Ravine from Hermit Hut

Needless to say, Tuckerman Ravine is a very dangerous area subject to avalanches and falling massive blocks of ice the size of automobiles. It also is very exciting and challenging for skiers and outdoor enthusiasts. The open porch of the Hermit Hut shelter is a great place to watch the skiers.

How do I get to Tuckerman Ravine?

Tuckerman Ravine can only be reached by hiking uphill - there is no ski lift, road, or method of access – other than to hike.
You start your hike (many wear their ski equipment on the hike) at Pinkham Notch to the Hermit Hut Shelter (http://timefortuckerman.com/tuckermanravinemap.html). Then you hike straight up the headwall of the Ravine, so you can extreme alpine, snowboard, or telemark ski your way back down. This video shows skiers on the Hillmans Highway, Left Gully, and Bowl.

Once reaching the Hermit Hut Shelter, extreme alpine, snowboard, and telemark skiers continue to climb another hour or so up to the headwall of the Ravine's various self-made ski lanes. This video shows skiers on the Hillmans Highway, Left Gully, and Bowl.

Microspikes or Crampons?

My video says we put on "crampons" on the trail. In fact we used "microspikes". To learn the difference go to Microspikes or Crampons? **(http://forum.hike-nh.com/viewtopic.php?t=5580)**. For most hikers in the Whites today, microspikes have replaced crampons - and some of the older hikers still refer to their crampons when they are indeed wearing microspikes.

A good reference for people for winter and spring travel is run by the Tuckerman Ski Patrol at www.mountwashingtonavalanchecenter.org. This site gives people information from November to Memorial Day on avalanche danger and snow/ski reports for Tuckerman and Huntington Ravines.

Figure 8 - Hillmans Highway and The Bowl

Figure 9 - Warnings and Views of Tuckerman

To see a graphic of various Tuckerman Ravine ski routes go to
Time for Tuckerman **http://timefortuckerman.com/routes.html**

Video Blog of Spring Hike to Tuckerman's
- **Tuckerman Ravine, Southeast Face of Mt. Washington, White Mountains, New Hampshire http://outdooradventurers.blogspot.com/2014/05/tucker man-ravine-southeast-face-of-mt.html**

A Mid-week Trek to Tuckerman Ravine

Figure 10 - Tuckerman Ravine Overlooking Hermit Hut

Today was a perfect time to hike to Tuckerman Ravine. In two hours Dundee, Dick and I made the three-mile uphill trip via Tuckerman Ravine Trail to Hermit Lake. The summer-like day was emphasized by Dick and I wearing t-shirts and shorts (we did have warm clothes in our backpacks for any change in weather.)

Tuckerman Ravine

Tuckerman Ravine, isolated on the east side of Mt. Washington in the White Mountain National Forest, is famous for its daredevil spring skiing, snowboarding, mountaineering, ice climbing and hiking. Moreover, Tuckerman's remoteness and its ever changing weather conditions and terrain can be dangerous – and even fatal. (http://www.tuckerman.org/tuckerman/tuckerman.htm)

If you are thinking of skiing Tuckerman, you should be an expert skier in good physical condition. The headwall at Tuckerman is between 45-55 degrees and the vertical drop is approximately 1200 ft. The only way to the top is by climbing the headwall. (http://www.out-there.com/tuckerman.htm).

Figure 11 - Skiers on Tuckerman

The hike started on a dry and bare rocky Tuckerman Ravine Trail. As we ascended to the middle section, we encountered snowmelt small streams crossing the trail, and we gingerly traversed slippery ice. The upper part of the trail was snow covered, and we could hear and see water flowing underneath our feet.

Fellow outdoor enthusiasts, carrying their downhill and telemark skis, boots and gear, passed us. Other hikers, like us, are there for the thrill of the surreal scene of this magnificent beautiful ravine with a reputation for beauty, avalanche danger, and untold climbing challenges.

Shared Thoughts:

• A trek to Tuckerman's is a perfect place to bond with your significant other, family, and friends. My wife Cathy and I have made this trek many times, and years ago, my son Tim and I encountered a sudden storm that nearly put an end to our lives. Memories of love, emotion, and bonding are part of my Tuckerman experience.

- 10:30 am temperature 82 degrees AMC's Pinkham Hut, 12:30 pm temperature 68 at base of Ravine.
- We were aware of an air and ground search for a 17-year-old Eagle Scout hiker who had been missing in this area since Saturday. At around noon we heard from a hiker the scout was found safe and in good condition.
- Camaraderie of all skiers was evident throughout the hike as we shared "where are you from", "conditions of your ski", "which side of the ravine did you ski?", and "Have you heard if they found the scout?"
- We wished a ten-year-old boy "happy birthday" after we learned he and his dad skied Hillman's Highway trail, the longest run in Tuckerman.
- We drank water every ten minutes to not get dehydrated. My backpack was filled with a quart of water, two peanut butter and jelly sandwiches, compass, map, duct tape, ace bandage, contractor trash bags for an emergency overnight, warm clothes, gaiters, winter hat, and gloves. We all wore hiking boots (wearing sneakers on this very rocky hike invites a sprained ankle and wet feet).

- After lunch at the caretaker hut, we started up the right section of the Ravine, but stopped because of rocks covered with slippery ice and brewing dark storm clouds moving swiftly over the headwall. Since storms come up quickly in this area, we did not hesitate to leave when we saw the threatening conditions.

Figure 12 - This trail ONLY if you are in top physical condition

Thinking of going to Tuckerman? Great, but before you go be prepared with a review of the HikeSafe program http://www.wildlife.state.nh.us/Outdoor_Recreation /hiking_safety.htm. The N.H. Fish and Game Department and the White Mountain National Forest have partnered up to create a mountain safety education program called "HikeSafe." A large component of the program is the Hiker Responsibility Code. The code applies to all hikers, from beginners on a short hike to experienced outdoor enthusiasts embarking on an expedition. Please practice the elements of the code and help the HikeSafe program spread by sharing the code with fellow trekkers. Creating an awareness of HikeSafe will help increase hiker responsibility and decrease the need for Search and Rescue efforts.

Dick, Dundee and I will never have to say, "We

wish we had hiked to Tuckerman's Ravine to watch the skiers and enjoy Tuck's majestic wilderness mountain scenery."

Video Reference Spring Hike to Tuckerman's
- Blog: Fantastic Spring Mid-week Hike to Tuckerman Ravine http://outdooradventurers.blogspot.com/2009/04/fantastic-mid-week-trek-to-tuckerman.html

Diana's Baths Waterfalls in Bartlett, New Hampshire

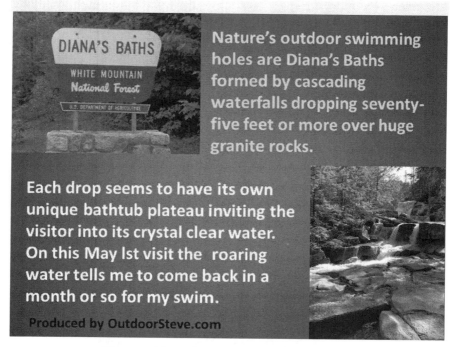

Figure 13 - Diana's Baths Waterfalls

Diana's Baths are Mother Nature's swimming holes and are a must see if you are in the North Conway area and want to experience nature at its finest. Diana's baths lie along Lucy Brook in Bartlett which is fed from Big Attitash Mountain. During the summer the baths are a great place for children and grown-ups alike to enjoy the tranquility of nature, and explore the many rocks, ledges, cascading falls and pools in the brook. The cascading falls measure close to 75 feet in total height.

The hike to Diana's Baths is a fairly easy 6/10ths of a mile on a relatively flat, wide gravel path. Being part of the US National Forest System, there is a large parking lot at the entrance to the hiking path.

References

- **Video and blog:** Diana's Baths Waterfalls in Bartlett, New Hampshire http://tiny.cc/wyh85x

- **North Conway Diana's Baths Waterfalls** http://www.northconwaynh.com/diana's-baths.html

Kayaking on Lake Coniston, NH

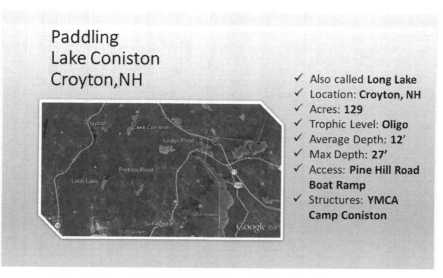

Paddling
Lake Coniston
Croyton,NH

✓ Also called **Long Lake**
✓ Location: **Croyton, NH**
✓ Acres: **129**
✓ Trophic Level: **Oligo**
✓ Average Depth: **12'**
✓ Max Depth: **27'**
✓ Access: **Pine Hill Road Boat Ramp**
✓ Structures: **YMCA Camp Coniston**

Figure 14 - Statistics on Lake Coniston

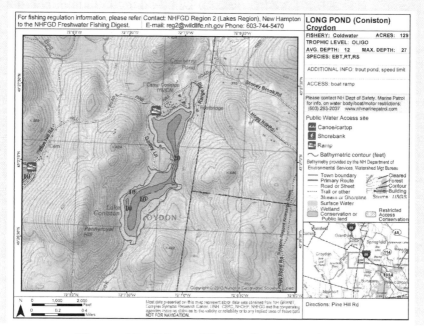

Figure 15 - Map of Lake Coniston Area

Figure 16 - The Dudley Lane Put-in

Figure 17 - Kayaking on Lake Coniston

Figure 18 – Loon Preening

Loons Preening & Bathing

You might think a loon is in distress when you see it preening or bathing, but these are actually important daily maintenance behaviors. I have even believed a loon was maybe dead because it appeared to be floating on its side with no motion minutes at a time – before it finally turned upright again. Here are some key points to help recognize these behaviors:

For loons, daily preening is a necessary maintenance behavior to keep their feathers aligned, waterproofed and in good condition. Individual feathers are like shingles on a roof; their interlocking structure creates a barrier so that water cannot penetrate their skin. Loons and other birds secrete oil from the uropygial gland (also called preen gland) at the base of the tail and work it through all of their feathers. This oil helps keep the feathers in place, like hairspray.

- A loon will often roll onto its side or back and start pulling the breast and belly feathers through its bill. One leg usually comes out of the water and the loon spins in circles while trying to reach these feathers.

- Since loons cannot reach their head and neck with their bills, they rub their head against their back or shoulders after secreting some oil from the preen gland.

- Loons will often flap their wings during and at the end of preening sessions. During a wing flap, a loon rises high up on the surface of the water and with neck outstretched, bill held high and wings spread, it will flap several times while shaking its head and neck.

- Tail wagging usually follows wing flaps. The loon holds its tail above the water's surface and shakes it from side to side, expelling excess water.

- Preening sessions can sometimes last more than 30 minutes.

Loon Bathing

Bathing is another maintenance behavior that is observed on a regular basis. Loons bathe to help get rid of feather parasites and clean their feathers.

- Bathing involves more vigorous splashing and submerging. A loon may completely roll over while thrashing in the water with partially opened wings.

- One or both wings are often seen flailing in the air and then are slapped back down on the water's surface.

- One or both legs may also be seen flailing in the air.

- A loon may dive backwards, flashing its bright white belly.

- It may intersperse splashing with dipping its bill and sometimes its head into the water to wash its face.

- Loons will often flap their wings during and at the end of a bathing session as well.

- Bathing sessions are often interspersed with periods of preening and may also last more than 30 minutes. A preening or bathing loon is a busy loon. Please make sure that you watch the action with a good pair of binoculars from a safe distance, so that your presence does not distract the loon from this essential part of its daily routine.

Loon Calls:

Northern New Hampshire is an area that enjoys the call of the loon – particularly early morning and late evening.

The Wail: The "Wail" is heard for many miles and is used to keep in contact with other loons on the same lake and surrounding lakes.

The "Wail" is most frequently given in the evening or at night, and can be heard for many miles. This haunting call is not an alarm call but is used to keep in contact with other loons on the same lake and surrounding lakes. The wail is a long, one, two, or three note call in situations where loons want to move closer to one another. Parents will wail to their chicks to encourage the chicks to leave the nest, to approach the parents when they have food, or to emerge from a hiding place. Listen to the "Wail".

The "Tremolo" has been described as "insane laughter"; it is 8 to 10 notes voiced rapidly which vary in frequency and intensity. This alarm call usually indicates agitation or fear, often caused by disturbance from people, a predator or even another loon. Members of a pair will also duet using tremolo calls. This is also the only call that loons make in flight. Listen to the "Tremolo".

The "Yodel" is only made by male loons. It is used to advertise and defend their territory, especially during incubation and chick-rearing. It's also used in territorial situations and aggressive encounters with other birds. Males will also yodel if a predator is seen that may be approaching the chicks, such as when an eagle flies overhead. Yodeling males crouch flat to the water with their head and neck extended and the lower bill just over the water. Listen to the "Yodel".

The "Hoot" call is not as intense or as loud as the other calls. It's a soft, short contact call between birds. Adults will hoot to their mates, and parents will hoot to chicks, enabling them to keep in touch with the whereabouts of the other birds. Adults also hoot to other adults of social groups residing on or visiting the same lake. Listen to the "Hoot".

References

- **Video and Blog: Kayaking Lake Coniston** http://outdooradventurers.blogspot.com/2015/07/kayaking-lake-coniston.html

- **Coniston NH Map** http://www.wildlife.state.nh.us/maps/bathymetry/coniston_croydon.pdf

- **The Loons Nest** http://www.loonsnest.biz

- **Loon Preening and Bathing** http://www.loon.org/preening-bathing.php

- **Loon Preservation Committee NH** http://www.loon.org/

Summer

I went to the woods because I wished to live deliberately, to front only the essentials of life, and see if I could not learn what it had to teach, and not, when I came to die, discover that I had not lived.
– Henry David Thoreau, Walden

Rowing through the eyes of a Beginner

Figure 19 - Lake Sunapee Rowing Club Lessons

"Never say I wish I had …" is an expression that has always motivated me. All summer I passed a road sign announcing, ***"Rowing Lessons Lake Sunapee Rowing Club. Next class starts August 3."*** I had watched snippets of racing shells on the Merrimack River, TV, and in summer Olympics. I decided this was my time to say, "Never say I wish I had rowed a shell".

Figure 20 - www.LakeSunapeeRowing.com

I spoke to a friend who I knew was taking rowing lessons with the LSRC – and she sent me the web site with a note of encouragement to join.

I registered for the Novice classes – three weeks of classes – three times a week – two hours each class. The LSRC provides the boats (also known as shells). Rowing is often referred to as **crewing**.

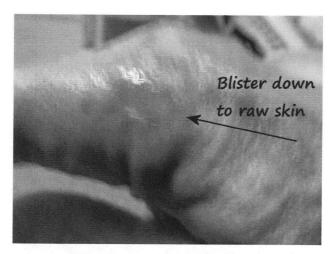

Blister down
to raw skin

Figure 21 - A Rowing Blister

Figure 22 - An 8+ Sweep with Mount Sunapee in Background

Our coach, Brenda, is just an amazing instructor with knowledge, skills, and a lot of patience. Brenda makes each class fun with personal instruction for each student, and a wealth of education on learning the language and techniques of rowing.

Enjoy the below video of this novice student and my classmates as we team and row together to never have to say, "I wish I had learned to row."

Figure 23 - Shoe Stretchers and Sliding Seat

Bedford Community **Television (BCTV)** is playing a 30 minute video (see below) detailing Steve's novice rowing experience. The dates and times of playing are published on BCTV. All community TV stations are welcome to use this video by contacting BCTV or by communicating directly with Steve.

The below references are shared for each reader's more intense research into the fascinating sport of rowing.

Distinction from other watercraft

"The distinction between rowing and other forms of water transport, such as canoeing and kayaking, is that in rowing the oars are held in place at a pivot point that is in a fixed position relative to the boat, this point is the load point for the oar to act as a second class lever (the blade fixed in the water is the fulcrum). In flatwater rowing, the boat (also called a shell) is narrow to avoid drag, and the oars are attached to oarlocks at the end of outriggers extending from the sides of the boat. Racing boats also have sliding seats to allow the use of the legs in addition to the body to apply power to the oar. Racing shells are inherently unstable, much like racing kayaks or canoes."

Two types of rowing

- In *sweep* or *sweep-oar* rowing, each rower has one oar, held with both hands. This is generally done in pairs, fours, and eights. In some regions of the world, each rower in a sweep boat is referred to either as *port* or *starboard*, depending on which side of the boat the rower's oar extends to. In other regions, the port side is referred to as stroke side, and the starboard side as bow side; this applies even if the stroke oarsman is rowing on bow side and/or the bow oarsman on stroke side.

- In *sculling* each rower has two oars (or *sculls*), one in each hand. Sculling is usually done without a coxswain in quads, doubles or singles. The oar in the sculler's right hand extends to port side, and the oar in the left hand extends to starboard side.

Figure 24 - LSRC Lessons include the Eight+, Quad Scull, Doubles, and Single

My first boat was a quad scull. A **quad scull** is a rowing boat designed for four persons who propel the boat by sculling with two oars, one in each hand. This four seater quad was 45 feet with a weight of 200 lbs. Its cockpit width is 20 inches. Our two oars were 9' each.

My second boat was a single scull one seater 24 feet in length, 75 lbs., and a 20 inch wide cockpit designed for a single person who propels the boat with two 9' oars, one in each hand.

My third boat was a double scull two seater, somewhat similar to a single scull but has two rowers.

My fourth boat was an Eight (8+) 65 foot shell with 8 rowers and a coxswain. We did what is called sweep or sweep-oar rowing where each rower has one 12 foot oar held with both hands. As each rower has only one oar, the rowers have to be paired so that there is an oar on each side of the boat. Sweeping is in contrast to sculling with my quad and single boats where a rower has two oars, one in each hand.

Some special attire is needed for rowing. Snug fitting shorts and shirts are best as loose fitting clothing could get caught in the oars and seat tracks. Compression type shorts are ideal. Dry socks are also a must. Socks should be synthetic or wool to help ensure that feet stay warm while wet and will help prevent blistering from the hull's shoes.

Personal Insights of a Novice Still Learning to Scull and Sweep

- As I was canoeing this week it hit me why canoe instructors always say, "Keep your paddle in the water during rough conditions." As sculling and sweeping oar blades in the water stabilized the boat, so does the canoe paddle blade!

- In canoeing and kayaking the paddlers face the bow. In sculling and sweeping rowers face the stern. Thus, the rower in the bow in the quad, double, and single need to frequently turn around to see where they are going. The bow person not only has to row, BUT has to make sure we are heading in the right direction and away from obstacles.

- In learning to row the instructor does not usually have everyone row at the same time. Initially I thought this was to give me a rest. Later I realized while not rowing I still had a critical task keeping my blades on the water to stabilize the boat for the other rowers.

- In the eight, quad and double if I made a mistake, the rowers stabilized the boat for me. In the single this was my responsibility - otherwise I would capsize.

Bedford Community Television (BCTV) has accepted the below 30 minute video detailing Steve's novice rowing experience. The dates and times of playing will be published shortly. All community TV stations are welcome to use this video by contacting BCTV or by communicating directly with Steve.

Below are references of some of the terms used in the video.

References

Video: ROWING through the eyes of a novice
http://outdooradventurers.blogspot.com/2015/08/rowing-through-eyes-of-beginner.html

Lake Sunapee Rowing Club
http://www.lakesunapeerowing.com

Glossary of Rowing Terms
https://en.wikipedia.org/wiki/Glossary_of_rowing_terms

Single scull
https://en.wikipedia.org/wiki/Single_scull

How to position hands on oars
https://www.youtube.com/watch?v=o3MdSkh2s2o

Rowing technique with diagrams on the rower
https://www.youtube.com/watch?v=W8a9nKkp1OM

Natural Rowing Technique
https://www.youtube.com/watch?v=9BAXGFwcVaY

Getting into a capsized single and double
https://www.youtube.com/watch?v=VYfvuXcSuqs

Recovery to Catch: How to Position Your Hands and Hold Your Oars
https://www.youtube.com/watch?v=o3MdSkh2s2o

Sweep Rowing
https://en.wikipedia.org/wiki/Sweep_(rowing)
Coxswain
https://en.wikipedia.org/wiki/Coxswain
Head of Charles Regatta
http://www.hocr.org/the-regatta/competitors/registration/

Lake Sunapee Rowing Club 2015 Flag Pole Race

The Lake Sunapee Rowing Club (LSRC) email announced their annual Flag Pole rowing race would be Sunday, August 23rd at Georges Mills from 6 am to 8 am. The boat categories would be singles, doubles, quads and eights. After the races there would be a pot luck breakfast at the beach.

This was an interesting email for competitive LSRC members, but there was no way I could consider any type of crewing competition. Certainly three weeks of rowing lessons was not supposed to make me a competitor.

After our weekly lesson on Tuesday, KC approached me and asked, "Steve, would you be my doubles partner in the Flag Pole race on Sunday?" Never say, "I wish I had …" crossed my mind, and I said "Yes, thanks for asking."

I did give KC an out option by saying, "If you can find a partner with more rowing experience please do so and I will completely understand."

To ease my restless nights before the race I was assured by KC, "Steve, it is really a very causal, friendly, and low-key competition."

Enough said. Enjoy the four minute video of Steve's and KC's participation in the Lake Sunapee Rowing Club Flag Pole Race.

References
- **Video: Lake Sunapee Rowing Club Flag Pole Race** http://outdooradventurers.blogspot.com/2015/08/lake-sunapee-rowing-club-2015-flag-pole.html
- Click ROWING through the eyes of a beginner http://tiny.cc/taqn6x to see Steve's earlier post on his rowing lessons.
- You can contact the Lake Sunapee Rowing Club at **http://www.lakesunapeerowing.com/**

Figure 25 - Steve and KC participate in the two person scull

Figure 26 - LSRC Members Celebrate the Race

Book Review for "The Boys in the Boat"

"The Boys in the Boat: Nine Americans and their Epic Quest for Gold at the 1936 Berlin Olympics"
by Daniel James Brown.
2013
ISBN 978-0-670-02581-7
A Number One New York Times Best Seller
Non-Fiction

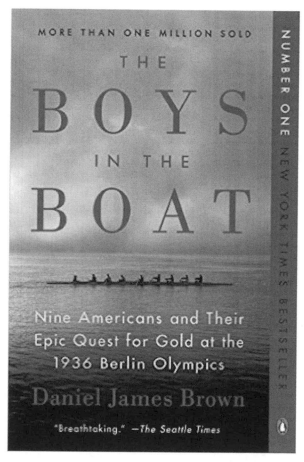

Figure 27- Book Cover – The Boys in the Boat

I just had to read *"The Boys in the Boat"* by Daniel James Brown. After taking three weeks of rowing lessons from the Lake Sunapee Rowing Club, then blog posting my rowing experiences - ROWING through the eyes of a Beginner and Lake Sunapee Rowing Club 2015 Flag Pole Race - and emails from friends strongly recommending the book, I felt I must read this *New York Times* Number One non-fiction best seller.

The Boys in the Boat documents in narration and story format how: nine college boys from the University of Washington - one coxswain and eight rowers; their coaches; and their shell designer; faced personal and political obstacles to stay in college, be on the non-scholarship rowing team, and get to the 1936 Berlin Olympics in Hitler's Nazi Germany.

The book not only tells the story of each person, but shares the historical and political significance of Hitler's Germany before World War 2.

Once into the book, I found myself relating to each character – and not being able to put the book down. Admittedly, I cried during the author's Epilogue.

To entice you to read this book here are excerpts from the book:

- George Yeoman Pocock: *"I believe I can speak authoritatively on what we may call the unseen values of rowing – the social, moral, and spiritual values of this oldest of chronicled sports in the world. No didactic teaching will place these values in a young man's soul. He has to get them by his own observations and lessons." (Chapter One page 7)*

- "Immediately after the race, even as he sat gasping for air in the *Husky Clipper* while it drifted down the Lager See beyond the finish line, an expansive sense of calm had enveloped him. In the last desperate few hundred meters of the race, in the searing pain and bewildering noise of that final furious sprint, there had come a singular moment when Joe realized with startling clarity that there was nothing more he could do to win the race, beyond what he was already doing. Except for one thing. He could finally abandon all doubt, trust absolutely without reservation that he and the boy in front of him and the boys behind him would all do precisely what they needed to do at precisely the instant they needed to do it. He had known in that instant that there could be no hesitation, no shred of indecision. Chapter Nineteen page 355

- The mantra M.I.B. "The initialization stood for *"mind in boat."* It was meant as a reminder that from the time an oarsman steps into a racing shell until the moment the boat crosses the finish line, he must keep his mind focused on what is happening inside the boat. The whole world must shrink down to within the small gunwales.... Nothing outside the boat – not the boat in the next lane over, not the cheering of a crowd of spectators, not last night's date – can enter the successful oarsman's mind." Chapter six Page 90

References

- **Blog: Book Review "The Boys in the Boat"** http://outdooradventurers.blogspot.com/2015/09/book-review-for-boys-in-boat.html

- Official Book Trailer https://www.youtube.com/watch?v=n58w0BctOvs

- Amazon.com The Boys in the Boat: Nine Americans and Their Epic Quest for Gold at the 1936 Berlin Olympics

I hope I have enticed you enough to read this well-written historical documentary.

Newbury Trail - Eagles Nest - Lake Sunapee Overlook

Mike and I were going to hike the Mt Sunapee Newbury Trail on Saturday. However, neither of us knew where the trailhead was – and the trail map we had was not clear. On Friday my wife and I scouted and located the trailhead in Newbury Harbor NH-103 west to the first left, then bear right on Lake Avenue to the trailhead sign on the right.

Figure 28 - Eagles Nest Overlook

The Trailhead sign in the blog video shows directly behind the Lakeview Avenue sign and jeep picture.

Figure 29 - Newbury Trailhead behind Jeep and Lake View Sign

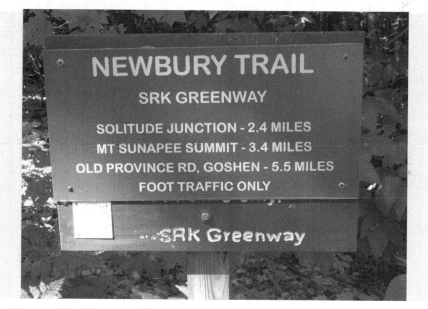

Figure 30 - Sunapee-Ragged-Kearsage Greenway Newbury Trail

We did a fairly easy two hour roundtrip hike to Eagles Nest overlook to a marvelous view of Newbury Harbor. The Eagles Nest overlook is a ten minute side-trail hike off the Newbury Trail. We met two trail maintainer volunteers working on the trail. They graciously answered my questions and demonstrated the moving and placing of a large rock. You can learn more about Cardigan Highlanders Volunteers Trail Crew at http://tiny.cc/7a631x

Figure 31 - Cardigan Highlanders Volunteer Trail Crew

Figure 32 - Yoga on the Newbury Trail

On Saturday Mike and I repeated the side trail hike to Eagles nest, and upon returning to the Newbury Trail we turned right continuing up the southern part of Mount Sunapee. This section of trail gets steeper and more strenuous to hike.

Figure 33 - Junction of Rim Train and Newbury Trail

We reached the Newbury-Rim Trail junction and then turned left staying on the Newbury Trail. For the next 10 plus minutes we climbed a rock-ladder laid trail. When we reached the Lake Sunapee overlook we had a magnificent view of the nearly 8 mile long by 2.5 mile wide Lake Sunapee and its many islands and main harbors. The sky was a bit hazy, but not enough to take away from this breathtaking sight.

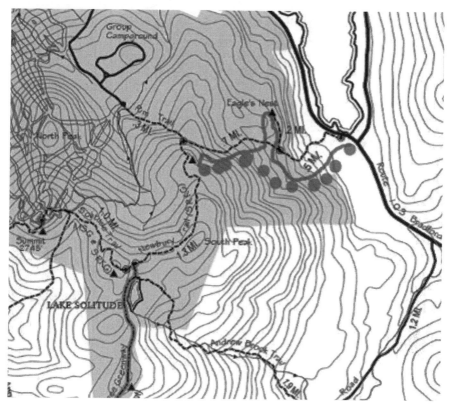

Hiking at Mount Sunapee

"The summit of Mount Sunapee (elevation - 2,743ft.) is reached via ski trails or the Summit hiking trail (Red Blaze). The start of the Summit Trail can be found on the right of the Lower Ridge ski trail, behind Sunapee Lodge.

A number of hiking trails are accessible year-round at Mount Sunapee. These include the Summit Hiking Trail, the Lake Solitude Hiking Trail and the Newbury Hiking Trail.

You may also hike on any of the ski trails during the summer months. **Ski trails are off limits for hiking during ski area operation, however, you are allowed to cross ski trails during winter operation to access the state hiking trails.** Please look uphill for downhill skiers and snowboarders before crossing the ski trails. Mt Sunapee snowshoe trails are located across the road from Spruce Lodge if you wish to have a shorter and less demanding hike."

For your safety be sure to be prepared when hiking:

- Allow ample time

- Wear sturdy footwear

- Know and heed weather forecasts

- Bring warm clothing and rain gear

- Bring food and water in with you

Mt Sunapee Maps & Info

- **Mount Sunapee State Park Hiking Trails**

- **Newbury Trail to Old Province Road, Goshen**

- **Sunapee-Ragged-Kearsarge Greenway**

- **Friends of Mt Sunapee**
  http://www.friendsofmountsunapee.org/cardigan-highlanders-announces-trail-work-on-mt-sunapee/

Lake Sunapee

"The lake is approximately 8.1 miles) long (north-south) and from 0.5 to 2.5 miles wide (east-west), covering 6.5 square miles with a maximum depth of 105 feet.

It contains eleven islands (Loon Island, Elizabeth Island, Twin Islands, Great Island, Minute Island, Little Island, Star Island, Emerald Island, Isle of Pines and Penny Island) and is indented by several peninsulas and lake fingers, a combination which yields a total shoreline of some 70 miles. There are seven sandy beach areas including Mount Sunapee State Park beach; some with restricted town access. There are six boat ramps to access the lake at Sunapee Harbor, Georges Mills, Newbury, Mount Sunapee State Park, Burkehaven Marina, and a private marina. The lake contains three lighthouses on the National Register of Historic Places. The driving distance around the lake is 25 miles with many miles of lake water views. The lake is 1,093 feet above sea level.

The lake's outlet is in Sunapee Harbor, the headway for the Sugar River, which flows west through Newport and Claremont to the Connecticut River and then to the Atlantic Ocean. The lake discharges about 250 cubic feet per second (on average), and the Sugar River drops approximately 800 feet on its 27-mile journey to the Connecticut River."

https://en.wikipedia.org/wiki/Lake_Sunapee

References

- Video and Blog: Newbury Trail to Eagles Nest to Lake Sunapee, NH
  http://outdooradventurers.blogspot.com/2015/09/newbury-trail-to-eagles-nest-to-lake.html

Four Days in Northern New Hampshire Hiking, Paddling, Tenting, and Moose Sighting.

Figure 34 - Welcome to New Hampshire "Live Free or Die"

Grab a cup of coffee or another favorite beverage, kick up your feet, and enjoy how a family bonds in the great north woods of New Hampshire. My 18-year-old nephew Austin graduated from his southern California high school. For Austin achieving this educational milestone, my wife, Cathy, and I arranged for him to fly to New Hampshire in July to experience our "Live Free or Die" outdoors.

The four day trip describes:
(1) Hiking Tuckerman Ravine Trail from the Appalachian Mountain Club's (AMC) Pinkham Notch hut to the AMC Lake of the Cloud (LOC) hut for a one night stay.
(2) Hiking from LOC hut to the peak of Mt Washington, the

highest mountain in the northeast at 6,288 feet and "Home of the World's Worse Weather".

(3) Tenting for two days at Lake Francis State Park in the Connecticut Lakes area of Pittsburg, NH.

- Hike to and around the 4th Connecticut Lake located on the border of Canada and the United States. The 4th Connecticut Lake is the headwaters of the 410 mile long Connecticut River

- Paddle the Third Connecticut Lake

- Paddle Lake Francis

- Moose sightings on 18 mile Moose Alley

In addition to Austin and me, our fellow trekkers were his father (my brother Dennis), my sons Timothy and Shaun, my two grandchildren 15 year old Madison and 12 year old Carson, Ron, my brother-in-law, and invited friends Justin and his 17 year old daughter Sarah. Ten would hike to the Lake of the Clouds (LOC) hut and Mt Washington, and seven of us would continue to the Great North Woods Lake Francis State Park campground.

Preparing the Hike to Lake of the Clouds Hut (LOC) and Mount Washington

As the hiking trek leader I had responsibility for the safety of my fellow outdoor enthusiasts:

- Which trail should we take?
  I had hiked Tuckerman's many times, and although Tuckerman's Ravine Trail is one of the most dangerous trails to LOC and Mt Washington, I wanted my group to safely experience the scenery, excitement, and knowledge of hiking this unique trail.

Figure 35 - View Overlooking Lake of the Cloud Hut

- What time in the morning do we start our hike to LOC? LOC serves their family style meals at 6 pm sharp (breakfast at LOC is 7 am sharp). I expected the hike from Pinkham to LOC to be between 4 and 5 hours.

- What kind of clothing, supplies, and food do we need for a one-day overnight hike in the White Mountains? Hiking Tuckerman Ravine Trail is not to be taken lightly. Snow, high winds, rain, lightning, and fog can be expected year round – this means ALWAYS prepare to spend the night on the trail in the mountains.

- What emergency supplies do we need in case of an unanticipated overnight while hiking?

    o AMC's Ten Essentials for a Safe Hike are mandatory. I enforced this by giving each person their own whistle and flashlight.

- For each person I provided a 3 mil / 30 gallon contractor bag (aka trash bag) in case we had to immediately camp on the trail (or daresay get lost for an overnight). To use this bag we would make holes in the corner of the bag for our eyes and mouth, slip the bag over the head, and have some level of protection.

- Duct tape. You never know when this can come in handy e.g. broken eye glass frame, sling, strap, etc.

You need to be in good physical shape for a five plus hour hike up Tuckerman's Ravine with sections nearly straight up (no need for climbing ropes), but certainly there are places where you use your hands to assist crawling up rocks. My training schedule included two hikes up Uncanoonuc Mt in Goffstown, NH. Uncanoonuc, combined with two months of four times a week speed walking four miles in my hiking boots, prepared me for Mt Washington, and in particular climbing the headwall of Tuckerman Ravine.

An Educational Dinner
Hmm, how do I emphasize the importance of hiking safety to teenagers? The night before our trip my wife Cathy made a great spaghetti dinner for Austin, Madison and Carson. This dinner was my opportunity to stress safety and necessary items for the hike. Unannounced, I demonstrated my hiking whistle (One toot for, "Where are you?" Two toots, "Come to me", and three toots, "Emergency".) I gifted to each a whistle and asked them to demonstrate a signal. Yes, they thought I was "loony", but indeed they practiced a lifesaving skill.

We spoke about hiking in groups. My son, Tim, has hiked with me many times and has my confidence in tight situations. He would lead one group up the mountain. Ron was also experienced, and he would lead another group. The sweep group (the slow hikers) would be led by me. Other than the aforementioned, no one was to get ahead of their leader – no matter what. We did not want to experience a lost hiker.

We cautioned about the importance of stopping every 10 to 15 minutes to drink water. An earlier hiking involvement, followed by a wilderness first aid course, made me realize dehydration can cause nausea and headaches and is easily avoided by frequent drinking of water. Mt Washington is a steep, long hike, and hydration is critical for our troop to completing a safe and enjoyable hike.

I emphasized **NO COTTON CLOTHING** – including underwear. I underscored this "strange request" by asking, "How long does it take cotton to dry out after getting wet?" In survival situations, cotton is known as "DEATH CLOTH." Cotton holds moisture instead of wicking it away from the skin, and when wet, cotton has zero insulating properties.

Pinkham Notch to Lake of the Clouds (LOC)

I had concern in guiding my group safely up to Lake of the Clouds. Years before when Tim and I took the Tuckerman Ravine Trail to Lake of the Clouds hut, we faced thick fog and could see only a few feet ahead. On that trek we used cairns, the rock piles used to designate the trail when above tree line, as the means to insure we kept on the trail. On this trip I needed to watch closely the expected Mt Washington area weather to be sure I did not put my party in danger if the weather report indicated severe conditions.

They say a picture is worth a thousand words. Enjoy the short **Video Reference** below of our hike up Tuckerman Ravine Trail to Lake of the Clouds Hut followed by a next day hike to Mt Washington.

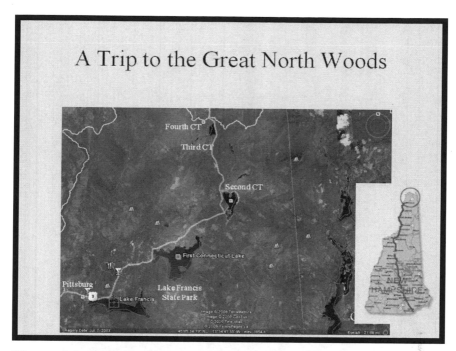

Figure 36 - The Connecticut Lakes of New Hampshire

The northern tip of New Hampshire has a pristine area known as the **Great North Woods.** I wanted Austin and my grandchildren to enjoy and appreciate this treasure of New Hampshire. Its many summer outdoor opportunities include paddling and fishing the Connecticut (CT) Lakes (Forth CT, Third CT, Second CT, First CT and Lake Francis), hiking around the Fourth CT, and Moose sighting.

Moose Sighting.

Figure 37 - Brake for Moose!

The moose is the biggest and most mysterious and majestic four-legged inhabitant of northern New Hampshire. Seeing a moose is always a thrill for me. Certainly for Austin and my grandkids, the thought of seeing these huge six to seven foot tall and 700 to 1200 pound animals was an expectation like waiting to get a glimpse of Santa Claus! There are 6,000 or so moose in New Hampshire and being in the Connecticut Lakes area in particular enhances the opportunity to see a moose. The last 18 or so miles on route 3 in Pittsburg is designated Moose Alley. Driving slowly on Moose Alley at 5 am also enhances your chance to see a moose. And, dusk is another good time.

What is the best way to find moose? My answer is always simple – look for cars pulled off alongside the road. For two days at dawn and dusk we drove very slowly up Route 3. See our moose sighting success in the below **Video Reference**.

The Republic of Indian Stream

Figure 38 - Group Hug at USA - Canada Boundary Marker

As we hiked to the Fourth Connecticut Lake I shared a history lesson not readily known. For a few years in the 1830s, an area of today's Pittsburg, NH was an independent republic, not part of New Hampshire and not part of the United States. The US attempted to tax the 360 inhabitants, and Canada tried to make them serve in its military, so the people decided to establish their own sovereign nation called, **The Republic of Indian Stream.** The existence of the Republic was ended by New Hampshire in 1835. Later, the Webster -Ashburton Treaty of 1842 established the border between Canada and the United States – the border markers that we would crisscross as we hiked to the Fourth Connecticut Lake.

Hiking the Fourth Connecticut Lake

The 78 acre Fourth Connecticut Lake is located on the USA/Canada border. It is called a "Lake", but in my mind is similar to a small bog or marsh. The narrow swampy walk around the lake took us a half hour. We stopped to take pictures at the outlet stream - the Fourth CT is the headwaters of the 410 mile long Connecticut River that ends in Long Island Sound. The trail to the lake starts at the United States-Canada customs border crossing station in Pittsburg, NH on the international border between the United States and Canada. The whole hike from custom station to lake, walk around the lake, a brief ten minute break, and the hike back, was less than two hours.

Paddle Third Connecticut Lake

Figure 39 - A Canoer on the 3rd Connecticut Lake

The 235 acre Lake is located about a half mile downhill from the

Fourth Connecticut. During our paddle on this pristine lake we saw beaver lodges and dams, loons, and the outlet to Second Connecticut Lake. Carson went for a swim. As we paddled around the northern end of the lake, we stopped to see the inlet from Fourth Connecticut Lake.

> **Video References Hiking, Paddling, Tenting and Moose Sighting in Great North Woods of NH**
> - **Blog: Four Days in Northern New Hampshire with Family and Friends Hiking, Tenting, Paddling, and Moose Sighting**
>   http://outdooradventurers.blogspot.com/2012/07/four-days-in-new-hampshire-of-family.html
> - **Hiking Tuckerman Ravine**
>   http://www.youtube.com/watch?feature=player_embedded&v=AkoJXIqB0kU
> - **Moose Sightings**
>   http://www.youtube.com/watch?feature=player_embedded&v=O-P__VJveeo
> - **Crossing Headwaters of 460 mile long Connecticut River at 4th Connecticut Lake**
>   http://www.youtube.com/watch?feature=player_embedded&v=dXM42H5KjuA

The Locks of the Trent-Severn Waterway

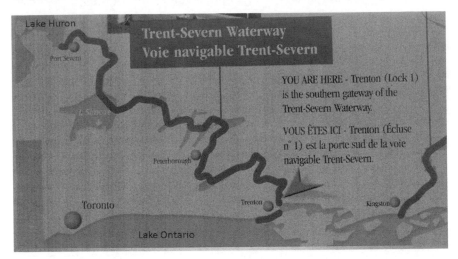

Figure 40 - Trent-Severn Map – Lake Ontario to Lake Huron

I found our Trent-Severn Waterway trip very difficult to make concise. Our Trent-Severn Waterway trek is so unique - such as our experience going through fourteen locks and living for eight days in a houseboat moving each day along the Waterway. With so much content, how do I describe all this and keep the discussion and videos under a few minutes?

The Trent-Severn Waterway is one of Canada's most spectacular waterways. The Waterway stretches 240 miles from Lake Ontario's Bay of Quinte to Lake Huron's Georgian Bay. My wife and I readily accepted an invitation to join our friends Linda and Dundee for a week on a houseboat on the Trent-Severn Waterway.

Friends have asked many questions such as, "What and where is the Trent-Severn Waterway?", "What was the houseboat like?", "What did it feel like going through a lock?", "How did you navigate?", and "Did you spend all your time on the houseboat?" I finally came to the conclusion I could only do this by breaking the trip into small videos and letting you choose for yourself which ones to view.

The waterway is an impressive chain of lakes and rivers linked by more than 40 locks and some 33 miles of excavated channels. All of the locks are situated in beautiful park-like settings and most are integrated within small and inviting villages. Indeed, the Waterway is a unique gem of Canada.

Figure 41 - Houseboat Waiting to Enter a Lock

Given the extensive length of the Waterway, our timeframe of eight days, and the need to return our rented houseboat to where we picked it up at **Happy Days Houseboats** in Bobcaygeon, Ontario, our trip would take us through only seven of the locks as we headed from Lake Ontario and turned around after we locked through Kirkfield Lift Lock. On our return we would repeat each of these seven locks.

Figure 42 - Our Houseboat Kitchen

The Waterway is home to two of the world's highest hydraulic lift locks, located in Peterborough and Kirkfield. Indeed, we locked the Kirkfield lift twice.

In addition, we visited via car four locks (Trenton, Glen Miller, Sydney and Peterborough Lift Lock). These visits gave us another perspective of the locks because at two of these locks the lock master allowed me into their lock houses to be an "associate" to work the controls to "lock in" and "lock out" the boats. I was even told by one lock operator, *"You are the oldest kid whoever assisted us!"* Indeed all the lockmasters and operators were wonderful.

The Lock Operators – Ontario Ambassadors

The lockmasters and operators who guide and oversee the locks as your boat passes through offer extraordinary assistance and indeed are ambassadors to Trent-Severn, Ontario, and certainly Canada. The warm welcome and support we received from them in going through the locks were exceptional.

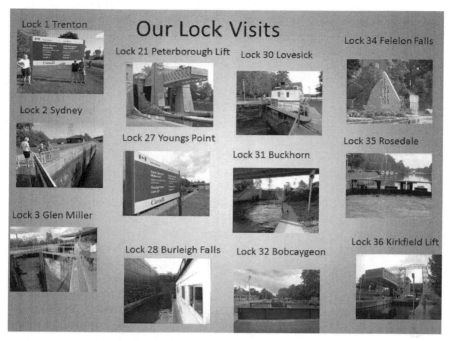

Figure 43 - Twelve Trent-Severn Waterway Locks

Each night we slept on the houseboat at designated areas outside the locks. One night we tied to trees on Wolf Island in Lower Buckhorn Lake with the back of the boat anchored in the lake.

The Trent-Severn includes fixed chamber locks and hydraulic lift locks. A lock is a device for raising and lowering boats between stretches of water of different levels on lake, river and canal waterways. The distinguishing feature of a conventional lock is it has a fixed chamber in which the water level is lowered or raised (as is the Bobcaygeon Lock); whereas in a boat lift lock, it is the chamber itself that rises and falls (such as the Kirkfield Lift Lock).

First, be sure to read the below **Seven Easy Steps for Locking Through**. Then, click on the two videos in the Videos Box below to see what it feels like to go through the **Bobcaygeon Lock** and the **Kirkfield Lift**.

"What Does It Feel Like Going Through a Lock?"

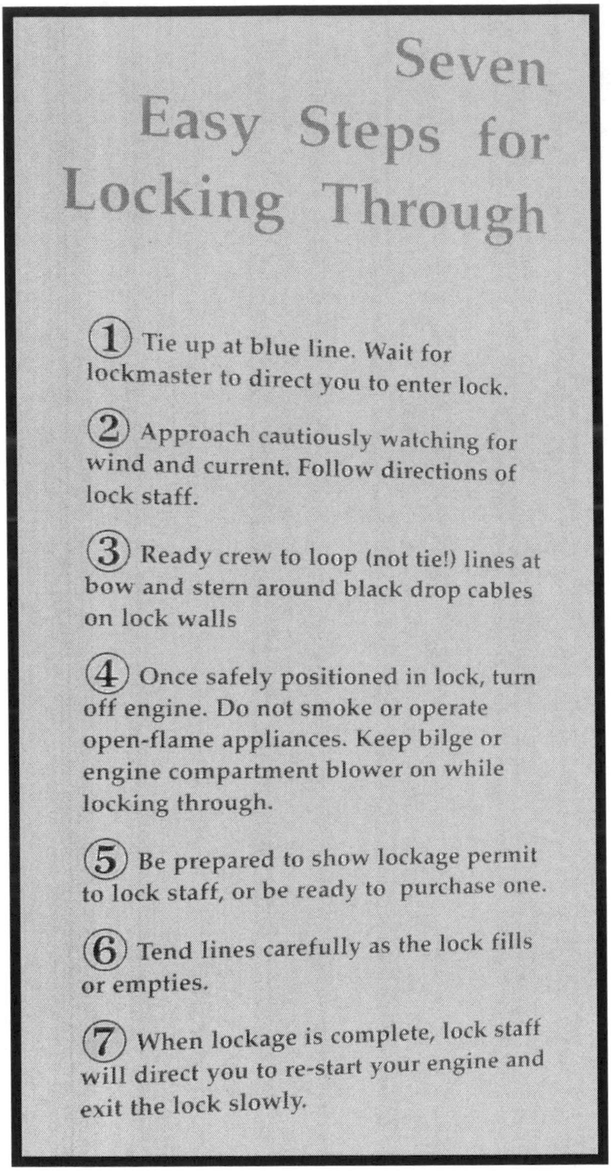

Seven
Easy Steps for
Locking Through

(1) Tie up at blue line. Wait for lockmaster to direct you to enter lock.

(2) Approach cautiously watching for wind and current. Follow directions of lock staff.

(3) Ready crew to loop (not tie!) lines at bow and stern around black drop cables on lock walls

(4) Once safely positioned in lock, turn off engine. Do not smoke or operate open-flame appliances. Keep bilge or engine compartment blower on while locking through.

(5) Be prepared to show lockage permit to lock staff, or be ready to purchase one.

(6) Tend lines carefully as the lock fills or empties.

(7) When lockage is complete, lock staff will direct you to re-start your engine and exit the lock slowly.

Figure 44 - Seven Easy Steps Sign Posted at All Locks

Navigation Aids and Tour Our Houseboat

We used navigational charts and a GPS to follow the Trent-Severn channel.

Figure 45 - The Pilot and Navigator Work Together

The houseboats are advertised for novice boaters, and the houseboat companies provide you (and require) an orientation course to include:

- Demonstrations on handling the boat (including docking it, starting/stopping) followed by each customer steering the boat thereby validating their hands-on abilities.

- Navigational skills to safely get you from here to there

- Location of all safety gear, onboard fire prevention, man-overboard procedures

- Channel markers, and river etiquette when overtaking and passing others (horn signals, etc.)

- A Final sign-off checklist of all things covered – and items located on the boat.

The entire training course is geared (before you cast off) to making your excursion a safe and rewarding adventure.

Personally, I recommend at least one driver feels comfortable in big boats. I would not recommend this trip for a complete boating novice by her or himself. Going through the locks, docking, and navigating requires boating experience.

Figure 46 - Our GPS - Where are we and how fast are we going?

My friend Dundee is a qualified boater on a variety of large boats. He is very comfortable with steering and navigating our 40 foot houseboat. Myself, I have a 19 foot deck boat, but admittedly it took me a while to calm my nerves on this "slow moving barge".

This was a large, slow to-turn boat. Initially, I was a bit nervous driving and navigating our 40 feet long and 14 feet wide houseboat into and out of the lock areas. Dundee's guidance and calming instructions certainly was a major plus for me when I was "Captain" of the boat.

History and Specs of The Trent-Severn Waterway
Construction began in the Kawartha Lakes region in 1833 with the lock at Bobcaygeon marking its beginning. It took over 87 years to finish the entire Waterway and only until after 1920 could a boat

travel the whole route between Lake Ontario and Lake Huron.

The navigation channel runs an average depth of six feet from start to finish. The conventional locks water level vary by 20 feet or less in raising and lowering boats, whereas the Kirkfield Lift is 49 feet and the Peterborough Lift is 65 feet.

Peaking at Balsam Lake the system takes the traveler 600 feet above Lake Ontario and 250 feet above Lake Huron's, Georgian Bay.

Standard lock dimensions are 120 feet long by 32 feet wide. The two exceptions are the Big Chute Marine Railway at 100 feet long by 24 feet wide and Port Severn at 84 feet long and 23 feet wide setting the limits if you wish to traverse The Trent-Severn Waterway from one end to the other.

"Did you spend all your time on the houseboat?"

There are many places to enjoy on the Trent-Severn and I cannot possibly discuss them all here. I will, however, refer to three that are special to me.

- The first is the *Buckhorn Canoe Company*. Dundee and I discovered this unique canoe building company owned and operated by Dick Persson.

  Dick's company builds, restores and outfits traditional all-wood, wood-canvas canoes, and small boats. We were immediately impressed with Dick's extensive historical knowledge of restoration of old watercraft, old canoe companies, and their boat and canoe models. His shop and showroom were museums unto themselves.

  Go to Dick's Blog (http://www.buckhorncanoes.com/) and read his passion and unique perspective for the history, research, building, repair, restoration, outfitting and use of wooden canoes.

  With Dick's permission I did a brief video of his comments on the differences between the Otter Tail and Beaver Tail paddles. Indeed, see the **Winter** section on using an otter tail to see if I improve my J-stroke by keeping my return stroke in the water.

- My next "must share" is my swimming in Burleigh Falls. I wanted so much to swim at least once on our trip, and this was my opportunity. The below Special Memories of Trent-Severn Waterway video has my brave five foot ledge jump into Burleigh Falls.

- Last, but not least, I strongly recommend a visit to the magnificent Canadian Canoe Museum (http://www.canoemuseum.ca/ in Peterborough, Ontario. This huge museum has exhibits and live hands-on demonstrations of canoe and kayak building. Found throughout the museum is the history of the native peoples of Canada and the historical importance that canoes and kayaks have played in the development of Canada's more remote wilderness areas.

  See a below brief video of special moments at the Buckhorn Canoe Company, swimming Burleigh Falls, and the Canadian Canoe Museum at the blog post.

Never Say, "I wish I had locked the Trent-Severn Waterway"

The Tent-Severn Waterway was a wonderful and memorable experience, and now Cathy, Linda, Dundee and I will never have to say, "We wish we had house-boated the Trent-Severn Waterway in Ontario Canada.

References to the Trent-Severn Waterway

- Trent-Severn Tool Kit
  http://www.trentsevern.com/newsite/

- http://en.wikipedia.org/wiki/Trent%E2%80%93Severn_Waterway

- http://www.thetrentsevernwaterway.com/#top

- http://www.ontariowaterwaycruises.com/kawartha.html

- http://www.thetrentsevernwaterway.com/
- http://www.happydayshouseboats.com

- http://www.buckhorncanoes.com

- The Waterway (Kawartha Region Lock Dimensions)
  http://www.thewaterway.ca/kawartha_locks.html

Videos Available for Trent-Severn Waterway
- **Outdoor Adventures Blog: The Trent-Severn Waterway**
  http://outdooradventurers.blogspot.com/2012/09/the-locks-of-trent-severn-waterway.html
- **Special Memories of Trent-Severn Waterway**
  http://www.youtube.com/watch?v=C6whLjZi_yw&feature=player_embedded
- **Bob Caygeon Lock**
  http://www.youtube.com/watch?feature=player_embedded&v=63tgMKffMp0
- Kirkfield Lock
  http://www.youtube.com/watch?v=SOAE3a-R0-w&feature=player_embedded

---

Paddling the Allagash Wilderness Waterway

A Father-Son Paddling Trek

Ten of us just returned from paddling the Allagash Wilderness
Waterway (AWW) in northern Maine. The ninety-eight mile
AWW is composed of streams, rivers, and lakes, and shines as the
brightest among the jewels of Maine's wilderness state parks and
historic sites.

This was a father-son trip with four dads and five sons. Linwood
"The Loon" Parsons (http://www.loonsnest.biz/) was our guide.
Loon's knowledge of the history and special sites around the
Allagash meant many side trips and informative lectures on the
unique history and lore of the Allagash Wilderness Waterway.

We entered the AWW at Indian Pond Stream on Saturday July
11th and exited Saturday July 18th at Allagash Village where the
Allagash River and the St John River meet.

Wildlife

Figure 47 - Shush...a Moose

A special treat for me was hearing the "snort" sounds of a moose. One evening a cow moose and her calf spent nearly an hour across the river from our camp, and we heard her many snort calls to her calf.

Each day we saw moose and we stopped counting moose at twenty-five.

Figure 48 - Look...There's an Eagle!

We saw many Bald Eagles, the national emblem of the United States and a spiritual symbol for native people. At one campsite a pair of eagles perched in trees across the river from our camp and made frequent screams as if warning us to stay away. We stopped counting eagles at ten pair.

A Loon Landing

A very unusual sight was seeing a loon land within a foot of our moving canoe. We spotted the loon coming toward us from afar, and we expected it to land. I have seen

Figure 49 - Experiencing a loon landing

73

loons land hundreds of time, but what was unique this time was the loon did not land, but kept approaching us head on. It kept coming and coming, as if it was going to collide with us.

The loon reminded me of seeing a seaplane coming in low and long with its proud chest up and no legs showing.

Finally, after much anxiety on our part thinking the loon did not see us, the loon smoothly settled within a foot of our canoe and became one with the water – all this without making a ripple. Wow! What a sight to see.

Chase Rapids

This was my son Tim's and my third trip into the AWW in six years, and the water level was the highest and fastest we had seen. My earlier trips required us to frequently exit our canoe due to the low water conditions. This time we fought headwinds on Eagle and Long Lakes. Chase Rapids are five miles of Class 1 and Class 2 rapids with many thrills. We did short stretches of class 2 rapids over Long Lake Dam and below Allagash Falls.

My biggest thrill was paddling with my son, Tim. We did the first three days with me in the stern, including Chase Rapids. On day four, we switched ends of the canoe for the remainder of the trek. Tim's ability to read fast moving water, along with his paddling strength, resulted in an adventurous, fun, and safe trip though the rapids. Our last day, the eighth, it poured rain, but since we were on our way out, the rain getting any of our gear wet was of no consequence.

Figure 50 - Eyes Focused Ahead in Chase Rapids

Figure 51 - Notice the Loaded Canoe with Camp Gear

Figure 52 - Time to Camp for the Night

Gourmet Meals

Figure 53 - Steak and Hot Dogs!

Our meals were simply delicious, well planned, and cooked by
"The Loon". Rib-eye steaks and potatoes cooked over our open
fire pit are just a sample of our eight days of gourmet dining. And
since one of the paddlers was a "hotdog eater", our chef
accommodated him for his own "special tastes".

Allagash History and Our Itinerary

Without a doubt, the Allagash Wilderness Waterway rates as one of the grandest wilderness areas east of the Mississippi. Its mystique draws canoeists from all over America and the world. First roamed by native Abenaki Indians in search of food and furs, then in the 1800's by lumbermen in search of virgin timber for logs and pulpwood, it is today visited by the adventurist paddler seeking a deep wilderness experience.

The Allagash Wilderness Waterway is rich in historical points of interest from those by-gone eras. It abounds in wildlife of every description, from the majestic Moose to the ubiquitous White-throated Sparrow. Extending some 98 miles end-to-end, the Waterway offers the canoer both lake and river paddling environments.

Our trip began at Indian Pond Stream, flowed into Eagle Lake, and then proceeded northward for eight days ending at Allagash Village on the Canadian border. "Pongokwahemook", an Indian name meaning "woodpecker place" and today called Eagle Lake, is a most interesting spot on the Allagash. We pitched our tents at Thoreau campsite on Pillsbury Island, the northernmost point reached by Henry David Thoreau in his expedition of 1853. It is from this base encampment that we launched our exploration of the "Tramway" that connects Eagle Lake with Chamberlain Lake and of the old locomotives that ran between Eagle and Umbazooksus lakes in the early 1900's lumbering era. A strange sight indeed to see these 90 and 100-ton locomotives sitting alone in this vast wilderness.

By now, everyone's paddling skills have become finely tuned and in two days or so, we will be running the canoes down famous Chase Rapids, a beautiful and exciting run of nearly 5 miles ending at Umsaskis Lake. As the river enters Umsaskis Lake it meanders through an attractive marsh where we see moose feeding on the plant life. Canada geese often stop over here on their great migrations up and down the Atlantic flyway.

We next cross Round Pond, the last pond on the Waterway and spend the next few days being carried along by the current through easy rapids as the Allagash River descends toward the Saint John.

Trout fishing at the mouths of the many brooks and streams offered Eric and Garrett the opportunity to wet a fly. That evening Garrett shared his 14" brook trout cooked over our campfire.

We portage the most awesome spectacle on the river; 40-foot high Allagash Falls, a thundering, boiling cauldron of power and beauty.

Figure 54 - Overlooking Allagash Falls

Fourteen river miles below Allagash Falls through class 1 rapids, the Allagash River delivers us back into civilization and our wilderness river adventure becomes a treasured memory.

A special notation on this trip. We had planned this trek two years ago, but one of the Dads was diagnosed with throat cancer. We had made all the arrangements, and two weeks before the trek, we had to cancel the trip as he began aggressive treatment. Two years later, cancer free, he and his two sons, made his Allagash Wilderness Waterway dream come true.

Never say, "I wish I had ..."

We now never have to say, "I wish I had paddled the Allagash Wilderness Waterway".

Figure 55 - A Father-Son Trip to the Allagash

For more information go to Allagash Wilderness Waterway http://www.maine.gov/cgi-bin/online/doc/parksearch/index.pl) and Maine Bureau of Parks http://tiny.cc/58l6sw

---

Video References for Allagash Wilderness Waterway
- Blog: Paddling the Allagash Wilderness http://tiny.cc/48ze5x
- Video of Pictures from Allagash Wilderness Waterway http://tiny.cc/vxze5x
- Videos of Paddling over Long Lake Dam, Allagash Falls, and Canoe Poling the Allagash http://youtu.be/7OANcEldsUA
- The Loons Nest http://www.loonsnest.biz

Ballad of the Allagash Wilderness Waterway

(To the tune of "Oh Lord, won't you buy me a Mercedes-Benz" by Janis Joplin)

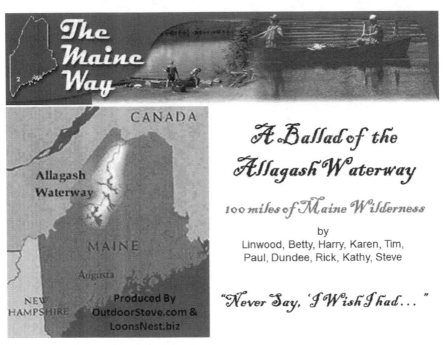

Figure 56 - Ballard of the Allagash by its Paddlers

Introduction
This Allagash Wilderness Waterway Ballad video was prepared from participants' memorable moments of expeditions guided by Registered Master Maine Guide Linwood Parsons and his wife Betty.

Without a doubt, the Allagash Wilderness Waterway rates as the gem of Maine's wilderness areas.

The Ballad of the Allagash Wilderness Waterway

(Kathy)
Oh Lord, won't you buy me a big can of Ben's.
I'm out in the woods now,
The flies never end.
Got bitten all over,
No help from my friends.
Oh Lord, won't you buy me a big can of Ben's.

Oh Lord, won't you buy me a bed of my own.
A mattress and box spring
That's not on the ground.
Last night I got bruises,
I slept on a stone.
Oh Lord, won't you buy me a bed of my own.

Oh Lord, won't you buy me a roll of TP.
Those baked beans of Betty's
Are getting to me.
Been wiping with leaves
Til I got poison ivy.
Oh Lord, won't you buy me a roll of TP.

(Linwood)
Oh Lord, won't you buy me a deputy's badge.
We helped save two druggies
At Little Allagash.
Ole Andy was naked,
And Tara was scared.
Oh Lord, won't you buy me a deputy's badge.

Oh Lord, won't you buy me new waterproof gear.
"Dry bags" became "wet bags"

When we sank to our ear.
We swam down the rapids
A chasin' the beer.
Oh Lord, won't you buy me new waterproof gear.

(Betty)
Oh Lord, won't you buy me a few more good years.
To paddle with Linwood
And Harry mit beers.
Chase Rapids with Karen
Without many fears.
Oh Lord, won't you buy me a few more good years.

(Karen)
Oh Lord, won't you buy me an instant campfire.
No sawing of firewood,
No stripping of bark.
No pleading with Linwood
Or Harry to lite it.
Oh Lord, won't you buy me an instant campfire.

(Harry)
Oh Lord, won't you buy me a brand new spruce paddle.
Chase Rapids are coming,
Excitement is high.
Cross draw, sweep, and a pry,
Til we all finished dry.
Oh Lord, won't you buy me a brand new spruce paddle.

(Steve)
Oh Lord, won't you buy me a Maine Master Guide.
To show us the Allagash,
In swagger and stride.
And teach us canoe rescue,
And a loon landing and more wildlife bona fide.
Oh Lord, won't you buy me a Maine Master Guide.

Oh Lord, won't you buy me a Chickadee and a Loon.
The breads in the Dead,
Cornish hens in the coffee can.
Folger's Black Silk,
and a pudding lid spoon.
Oh Lord, won't you buy me a Chickadee and a Loon

Oh Lord, won't you buy me a campsite to rest.
Spruce gum for the rookie,
Counting moose at its best.
A swim though the rapids,
Flint and steel for our test.
Oh Lord, won't you buy me a campsite to rest.

Oh Lord, won't you buy me a Long Lake Dam
A dam to portage if you can,
Or paddle at risk and I'll be dam.
A spike waiting to rip the canoe,
Tim and Steve paddled be dammed.
Oh Lord, won't you buy me a Long Lake Dam.

(Tim)
Oh lord take me down to the Allagash now.
Take me to the north woods,
Where the moose runs wild and proud.
To see the eagles soar,
As I relax on the shore.
Oh lord take me down to the Allagash now.

Oh Lord, won't you buy me some rapids right now.
The "V" through the rocks
will guide us somehow.
The draw stroke shall save us
with a quick turn of the bow.
Oh Lord, won't you buy me some rapids right now.

Oh Lord, won't you buy me more beer.
To help me create more cairns made of stone,
And the whistles of willow,
And the white birch bark stars.
So much more to create, so
Oh Lord, won't you buy me more beer!

(Paul)
Oh Lord, won't you buy me a big ole white sail.
I'm on Eagle Lake and,
The wind never fails.
My arms ache from paddlin',
Oh, S#%t is that hail?
Oh Lord, won't you buy me a big ole white sail.

(Linwood)
Oh Lord, won't you buy me a big ole fat fish.
I'll gut him and skin him,
Then he'll land in my dish.
An eighteen inch Brookie,
Now that'd be my wish.
Oh Lord, won't you buy me a big ole fat fish.

Oh Lord, won't you buy me a bigger Canoe.
'Cause the one I have now,
Just simply won't do.
Need more room for the beer,
for the hard strokin' Crew.
Oh Lord, won't you buy me a bigger Canoe.

(Rick)
Oh Lord, won't you buy me some stars in the Sky.
They look near at hand,
yet, are so high.
I'm just a lightening bug seeking a mate,
in the heavens above, but I'm feeling spry.

Oh Lord, won't you buy me some stars in the Sky.

(Steve)
Oh Lord, won't you buy me paddlers so grand.
Dundee is prepared,
And navigates first hand.
Timothy skilled in the stern,
When the river gets tough he insures the turn
Oh Lord, won't you buy me paddlers so grand.

Oh Lord, won't you buy me a campfire recipe.
Garret flint and steel,
Tim saws wood fire-to-be.
Linwood's cuisine is five-star,
Lobster and eggs benedict are the par.
Oh Lord, won't you buy me a campfire recipe.

Oh Lord, won't you buy me "Never say I wish I had …"
For eight days we were in awe of the Allagash and the Loon,
Our skills grew as we paddled in tune.
Coolers with names of rivers,
All are lifetime of memories delivered.
Oh Lord, won't you buy me a "Never say I wish I had …"

References

- **Video Blog**: The Ballard of the Allagash Wilderness Waterway **http://tiny.cc/s7d44x**

- Tim Priest Reflects on Treks Guided by Loon Parsons **http://tiny.cc/y9d44x**

- The Allagash Wilderness Waterway: A Father-Son Paddling Trek http://tiny.cc/wbe44x

- Nine videos of the Allagash **http://tiny.cc/see44x**

Tim Priest Reflects on his Maine Paddling Treks Guided by Linwood "The Loon" Parsons

Figure 57 -Tim Reflecting on Linwood and Betty

Tim Priest Reflects on his Maine Paddling Treks Guided by Loon Parsons (http://tiny.cc/y9d44x) is a recently identified video made by Frank Crosby as he interviewed Tim Priest heading for eight days of paddling and tenting on the 92-mile North Maine Woods Allagash Wilderness Waterway in July 2009. We call this particular trek a *Father-Son trip* as the expedition of ten was made-up of four Dads and their sons and one friend.

Tim has been on many wilderness paddling trips guided by Master Maine Guide Linwood "The Loon" Parsons and his wife Betty "The Chickadee". Tim shares his reflections on Linwood and Betty and his Maine North Woods trips.

The video (http://tiny.cc/y9d44x) includes pictures from the Father-Son Allagash Wilderness Waterway trek.

Figure 58 - Chickadee and Loon Parsons

Thank you to Frank Crosby for sharing this interview.

References

- Video and Blog: Tim Priest Reflects on his Maine Paddling Treks Guided by Loon Parsons http://tiny.cc/y9d44x

- Paddling on the Allagashh Wilderness Waterway http://tiny.cc/wbe44x

- http://www.outdoorsteve.com

- The Loons Nest http://www.loonsnest.biz

- The Ballad of the Allagash Wilderness Waterway http://tiny.cc/s7d44x

Hike Grand Canyon Bright Angel Trail Down to Indian Garden and Back to the South Rim

Figure 59 - Bright Angel Trail

Last summer I had the privilege of being in Grand Canyon National Park in northern Arizona. Certainly as an outdoor enthusiast, I had to walk more than the Canyon's Rim Trail. My friend JK recommended a hike into the Canyon to Indian Garden via the Bright Angel Trail. The estimated hiking time was 6 to 9 hours for this 9.2 mile hike down and back to the south rim.

My enthusiasm for hiking into the Canyon was cautioned by my fears of:

1. My fear of height. The south rim of the Grand Canyon is nearly 7,000 feet above sea level. The thought of looking over a drop-off of thousands of feet was admittedly something I was not sure I could face.

2. Meeting Mules on the Bright Angel Trail. There are frequent mule trips passing hikers on Bright Angel Trail. Could I squeeze close enough to the mountain side to let mule riders pass me on the Trail?

Figure 60 - "Mules ahead" is Common on Bright Angel Trail

3. Width of the Bright Angel Trail. Would the Trail down into the Canyon be so narrow as to force me to hug the mountain?

4. On Thursday morning at 6:40 am I began my hike on the south rim at the Bright Angel Trailhead. Two and a half hours and 4.6 miles later I reached Indian Garden. The hike down was fabulous, and I stopped frequently in awe of this incredible landscape and to take pictures and "smell the roses" of my America's beautiful country.

The four ½ hour return trip from Indian Garden to the rim was quite the challenge. The only thing that kept me going was I knew I had a six-pack sitting on ice in my cooler!

Figure 61 - Looking Up from Indian Garden

I believe the main reason for my exhaustion on the return trip from Indian Garden to the south rim was because I had not trained at 7,000 feet above sea level. My daily Bedford, New Hampshire training runs were at an elevation of 275 feet.

Lessons learned from my six plus hour hike from the south rim on Bright Angel trail to Indian Garden were:

• Height. My fears were for naught. The width of the trail was four to six feet, and most often the cliff side of the trail had trees and rocks that eliminated any fear of falling hundreds or thousands of feet

• The width of the trail was more than enough to accommodate mules passing. I had three groups of mule riders pass me on the way up. As they passed I simply sat on the mountain side with plenty of room to relax, drink water, and take pictures, as you will see in the video.

• The three rest areas (Mile-and-a-Half Resthouse, Three-Mile Resthouse, and Indian Garden) all had water sources for refills of my water bottles.

• The dust from the limestone was choking and blinding. Following another hiker up the trail put me in a dust cloud and I had to wait until the hiker was way ahead before I continued my trek. The mules passing generated even more dust. Certainly a person with breathing issues needs to be very aware of this situation.

• Shade was plentiful in my morning trek down. However, my journey back to the rim started around 10 am and shade was less prominent and the bright sun was hot, resulting in sweat mixed with suntan lotion (a mandatory item) burning in my eyes.

• There were four-foot timbers every three to four feet on the trail to prevent trail wash away. This meant on the return to the rim I had to constantly lift my feet six to twelve inches with every step. My thighs began aching before I reached the Three-Mile Resthouse.

• My approach to the hike back was to divide my trek into three phases: (1) Hike from Indian Garden to the Three-Mile Resthouse, (2) Hike from the Three-Mile Resthouse to the One-and-a-Half-Mile Resthouse, and (3) Hike from the One-and-a-Half-Mile Resthouse to the Canyon's rim.

There are over 200 heat-related rescues in Grand Canyon National Park each year, and most of them on the Bright Angel Trail. So, a word to the wise.

Down is Optional – Up is Mandatory

Hmm, I trust the below picture of **Down is Optional, Up is Mandatory**, will cause you to ask yourself, "What does **Down is Optional – Up is Mandatory** mean?" Well, as noted, hiking down the Canyon can be essentially an easy stroll. Your main concern is to lift your feet so as not to trip over the log sections and rocks. Thus "Down is Optional" means go down the canyon knowing you must be able to climb back up – thus "Up is Mandatory" means you are responsible for getting yourself back up to the canyon rim.

Figure 62 - Sign at Three-Mile Resthouse

"**Up is Mandatory**" means **BEFORE** you go further down into the Canyon you must understand and accept all the barriers that can prevent you from later returning to the rim.

Here is an incomplete list of barriers to making a safe return to the rim (which is 7,000 feet above sea level):
- Your body must be at a good level of cardio fitness.
- You will be returning up the same 4.6 mile trail – and that distance in itself can be difficult.
- The climb back to the upper rim means the constant lifting of your legs and the hurt of your thighs.
- Minimal shade.
- Constant clouds of dust from the path and certainly when mule trains pass – you will be breathing dust into your

lungs – even if wearing filtering scarfs.
- You must stay hydrated – means constantly drinking water.

Thus, the choice to go DOWN is a life-threatening decision made BEFORE you leave the top.

The steep plunge is made somewhat easier through switchbacks curling down the mountain. The need to replenish water is a lifesaving concern in a desert environment. Water replacement in May is no issue as my 4.6 mile descent of the Bright Angel Fault to Indian Garden had three springs. Only Indian Garden has water year-round. You still need to carry your own water – and constantly replenish at each water stop.

Memorable Moments

• As I hiked I began thinking this trail would be runnable, similar to my winter wild experience described here in an earlier blog post. Then, just before the One-and-a-Half-Mile Resthouse, I was passed by a person running. A few minutes later I met him at the Resthouse. We introduced ourselves, and he said he was 63 years old and "out for an early morning run". He turned around at this point and ran upward toward the rim.

• As I neared Indian Garden the trail leveled off, and I would run a bit – both to reduce the time to Indian Garden as well as to change my gait and vary the use of different leg muscles.

• On my return to the rim, I could see a woman walking very slowly in front of me. She was stumbling and stopped frequently to grasp the wall. She appeared to me to be in trouble. I caught up with her, and we spoke as we rested against the wall. I asked her if she needed any assistance, and she replied "No". We both were near finishing, and I waited for her near the Bright Angel Trailhead. We did a high-five. Certainly she was close to not understanding, "**Down is Optional – Up is Mandatory**"

• Because of my early morning start, almost my entire down hike was in the shade. However, my return hike was mostly in the sun - and it was very hot.

• Going down I did not touch the wall. On my trek back, I frequently would use the wall to help support my upward progress - and the wall was cool. I kept thinking a hiking stick would be nice about now.

Enjoy my video and hike into the Grand Canyon to Indian Garden and my return to the south rim.

I never have to say, "I wish I had hiked Bright Angel Trail into the Grand Canyon"

See all my below **Video References** for pictures and videos of the Bright Angel Trail hike.

References to the Bright Angel Trail

• http://en.wikipedia.org/wiki/Bright_Angel_Trail

• http://www.bobspixels.com/kaibab.org/bc/gc_tr_ba.htm

• America's 10 Most Dangerous Hikes - Bright Angel Trail, Grand Canyon, AZ

- **Blog: Hike Bright Angel Trail**
  http://tiny.cc/54bc6x

- **Hike on Bright Angel Trail**
  http://tiny.cc/i6bc6x

Sea Kayaking and Camping on the Maine Island Trail

My cousin Linwood suggested I join the Maine Island Trail Association (MITA). (http://www.mita.org/) The Maine Island Trail (MIT) is a 375-mile chain of over 180 wild islands along the coast of Maine. The MIT is a must do for any outdoor enthusiast.

The Planning Phase

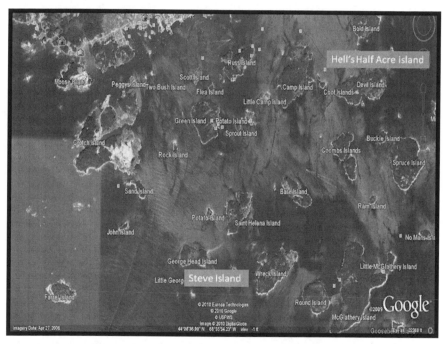

Figure 63 - Maine Island Trail Map of Our Trip

Kayaking and camping on islands in the Atlantic Ocean is not something one does on a whim. Who would like to go with me? When do we go? Where do we put-in? Where do we park the car for three days? Which islands do we camp on? Do we need fire permits? Do we need camp site reservations?

MAINE ISLAND TRAIL
O N L I N E G U I D E

I invited my regular camping and paddling buddies, and Dundee was the sole positive responder. Dundee and I selected Stonington on Deer Isle as our put-in because it offered a plethora of islands close to shore for our maiden trip.

I emailed the office of the Maine Island Trail Association with questions:

- **Island fire permits** - There is a telephone number in the MITA app (http://www.mita.org/app/) and hard copy guidebook (http://www.mita.org)
- **Camp site reservations** -There is no need for camp reservations on any of the islands - a MITA member has access to all sites on the trail, at any time, unless the guide descriptions indicates otherwise)
- **Put-ins available** - The Deer Isle overview page of the guide has a list (we selected Old Quarry Ocean Adventures **http://www.oldquarry.com**)

Linwood sent emails on maps (http://www.charts.noaa.gov/OnLineViewer/13313.shtml) for nautical navigation charts. He cautioned us to plan transits from the islands and mainland using a favorable following tide flow. Tides can be 2 to 4 knots in some of those channel passages, and if we end up bucking the tidal flow, we won't make much headway toward our destination and may run out of energy and/or daylight.

He sent us tide charts (e.g. http://www.maineboats.com/tide-charts/tides?t=augstn10) as tide knowledge is critical for camp sites and campfires, since the fires must be below the high tide line. The velocity of flow is maximum at mid-tide and slackens toward either end, reaching null at the direction of change. In the Stonington areas the tide will run about 12 feet (give or take the phase of the moon effects). We needed to remember to drag our kayaks a boat length or two above the high tide mark. When the tide rises 12 plus feet, we do not want to find our transportation has gone out to sea.

Figure 64 - A Good Navigator with a Map and Compass

Our gear included compasses, relevant guides and charts, the MITA guidebook, and a plastic water resistant nautical chart.

Packing our kayaks for our three day paddle meant tough decisions on what to bring and what to leave. My wife Cathy thought we would never pack the gear we had readied, but indeed we managed without sinking our kayaks.

Our Itinerary

Hells Half Acre Island on Wed Night and Steves Island on Thurs Night with a 4 pm Fri Return to Old Quarry.

**Figure 65 - Our Put-In at Stonington, Maine, Located on the
Southern Portion of the Island of Deer Isle.**

I sent emails to friends to follow our progress on their email with
Google Maps (the app is called **Where's My Droid**
(http://www.wheresmydroid.com/). I also downloaded an app
called **My Tracks** (http://www.mapmytracks.com/) to follow
our island trail paddle.

Day 1 – Wednesday

We registered our itinerary with Old Quarry. The Old Quarry staff
were extremely accommodating with information on selecting
alternative islands to camp on (e.g. "too buggy", "be careful of
lobster boats when crossing channels and between islands", etc.)

Figure 66 - Old Quarry Ocean Adventures

We had a smooth put-in at Old Quarry, and with a smooth paddle we were at Hells Half Acre island in just over thirty minutes. We were in awe of the island and the view of the bay. We took a walk about this two acre island, and located a nice spot on the east end of the island and pitched our tents on two wooded platforms.

Our initial plan was to save a camping spot by pitching our tent, and then doing some paddling to other islands. However, we were in awe of this paradise, and after some adult beverages, we decided to cool it for the night right where we were. This proved to be the right decision as shortly after we landed a three masted schooner, the "Victory Chimes", with five sails full, tacked into our harbor. It was a magnificent sight.

Figure 67 - "Victory Chimes" from Hell's Half Acre Island

Dundee was chief chef for this evening's dinner. We made a campfire below the high water line, and he proceeded to prepare beans and franks. Fabulous meal.

The sunset was dreamlike on this beautiful summer evening with a gentle breeze.

On Wednesday night we went to sleep surrounded by beautiful islands with clear skies and overhead stars.

Day 2 – Thursday

We awoke Thursday morning on an island in the middle of the ocean! We were completely engulfed in pea soup fog!

We had a lazy breakfast hoping the fog would clear. It did not.

At 10 am we decided to use our map and compass skills, and find our way to Steves Island. Dundee's experience at reading a nautical chart and steering by compass were impressive.

Figure 68 - The Fog

I felt comfortable with Dundee leading the way, but I must admit it was a weird feeling paddling into pea soup fog and hoping to find our next marker to know we were on course to Steves Island.

It took us about an hour to paddle to Steves from Hells Half Acre, as we meandered between a few islands enjoying this surreal experience of fog paddling. We could see about thirty feet ahead, so when we located an island, we paddled around it so as to take in the scenic pleasures of the spruce and granite topography along its shoreline, and if truth were to be told, to be sure we could recognize the island on our navigational map so we knew where we were.

Figure 69 - Paddling Away from Hell's Half Acre Island

When we found Steves Island, we were met by a couple, Taylor and Catherine, who had spent the prior night there, and because of being fog bound today, they intended to spend another day on Steves trusting that Friday's sun would burn away the fog.

We found a delightful campsite to pitch our tents. We toured this rock bound island, with balsam trees in the middle. Of course with the fog, our views off the island were essentially nil. We could hear lobster boats, but did not see them.

During the day, four kayakers in beautiful hand-made sea kayaks found the island for lunch. Interestingly, I knew one of the kayakers, so it was fun talking old times. They had all the appropriate navigation equipment for foggy weather, and after lunch left to make their way back to their campsite at another MITA Island.

A Fresh Mussels Feast

Given we were now friends with Taylor and Catherine, we invited them to join us for Steves Island fresh mussels and pre-dinner Hors D'Oeuvres. The **Video References** box below offers a link to our ocean mussels feast.

Figure 70 - Mussels Bed at Low Tide at Steves Island

Figure 71 - Steves Island and Steamed Mussels

Day 3 Friday

We awoke at 5:30 am Friday hearing the working lobster boats getting an early morning start. The fog was lifting and we knew the day would be clear. Around 9 am we began to be surrounded by views of the islands, as indeed they had been depicted on our map.

Figure 72 - An Early Morning Working Lobster Boat

At 10 am we started a gentle paddle back to our Old Quarry take-out via Crotch Island and Stonington. We left Steves Island with wonderful memories of ocean mussels and new and old friends. Crotch Island used to be a stone quarry, and was loaded with monstrous granite cut stones. A lot of the granite blocks used in the construction of many government buildings and monuments in our nation's capital were mined off this island.

We paddled along the shorefront of Stonington harbor, and around 1 pm we pulled into our take-out.

We reported our return at the **Old Quarry Ocean Adventures** office, and after buying three freshly caught Maine lobsters, we headed home to New Hampshire.

Shared Learning

• My Droid Incredible ran out of power in less than 7 hours after its full charge, so my expectations for **Where is my DROID**, and

105

My Tracks was a big negative (although some friends used GPS My DROID on day one and it worked great.

• Always bring a water resistant nautical map and compass – and certainly know how to use it BEFORE you go

• Join the Maine Island Trail Association (MITA)

• Most assuredly I will return many times to enjoy and explore the 200 plus islands cared for by the Maine Island Trail Association (MITA) membership.

• Enjoy the below **Video References** taken on MIT

• Never say, "I wish I had paddled the Maine Island Trail"

Video References Paddling the Maine Island Trail
  • Blog: Sea Kayaking on the MIT
    http://outdooradventurers.blogspot.com/2010/08/sea-kayaking-and-camping-on-maine.html

  • Hells Half Acre's Island Pea Soup Fog
    http://www.youtube.com/watch?v=k4G4KmqLIp8&feature=player_embedded
  • Eating Ocean Mussels on Steves Island
    http://www.youtube.com/watch?v=NhfMKal5DWo&feature=player_embedded
  • Old Quarry Ocean Adventures
    http://www.oldquarry.com/
  • Maine Island Trail Association
    http://www.mita.org

Ocean Kayaking in the Deer Isle Region of the Maine Coast – Stonington to Isle au Haut

The Deer Island Region of the Maine Island Trail

The Maine Island Trail (MIT) is a 375-mile chain of over 180 wild islands along the coast of Maine. In mid-July friends Dundee, Cully, David and I did a three day paddle on the MIT in the Deer Island Region. The Deer Isle Region extends from Stonington south to Isle au Haut and east into Blue Hill Bay. We tented two days on the two acre Steves Island (name by coincidence.)

We put-in at Stonington, Maine at the Old Quarry Ocean Adventure campground. See the video below for exciting footage of our trip, including a Google Earth map of our MIT route.

Photo by Randy Hess
Steves Island, Maine
July 22, 2014

Figure 73 - Steves Island Campsite

Special notes on our trip

- **Over the years, the pronunciation** of "Isle au Haut" has drifted considerably. Nowadays, people who have spent time on the island pronounce it "i-la-HO."

- **Dundee was both our Chef and Navigator**. He is top-notch in both areas.

- **Where are we in the Atlantic?** A map and compass are mandatory in this Deer Island area consisting of a 40 offshore island archipelago.

Figure 74 - Packing Kayaks from Quarry Ocean Adventures

Admittedly we had moments where we were questioning the name of the islands we could see in the distance. Certainly, when fog is present (frequently), you either stay on a known island, use your map and compass to get to your next island destination, or back to the mainland.

- **Disposal of human waste**

  o The Maine Island Trail Association (MITA) requests all island visitors carry off solid human waste and dispose of it safely on the mainland. The Maine Island trail Guide lists several good carry off methods to help you deal with human waste on the Trail. We chose the Crap Wrap method.

Figure 75 - All Trash is Carried Out

- **Water**

  - We brought our own potable water. The islands we visited had no drinking water - and remember, we were in the ocean.

- **Day 1 Old Quarry Campground to Steves Island**

  - A 4.6 mile paddle from Old Quarry Ocean Adventures campground to the 2 acre Steves Island where we camped for two nights

  - Met Randy and son Steve from Lancaster, PA

  - First come – first camp. Steves Island 2 acres and three sites – ten max occupancy

  - Put-in and parking at Old Quarry Adventure Campground

  - 90 plus minute paddle from Old Quarry to Steve's Island.

  - Dave caught mackerel (cooked over campfire.

Figure 76 - Map Quarry Ocean Adventures to Steves Island

- **Day 2 Steves Island to Isle au Haut and return**

  o Day starts with Chef Dundee cooking McNestlers for breakfast.

  o 11 mile round trip paddle from Steves Island to Isle au Haut. The paddle trip was close to 5 hours with gusts of wind and choppy seas.

    • Went ashore at Harbor Island.

    • Paddled by Merchant Island, Pell Island, Nathan Island to the Isle au Haut Thoroughfare.

110

- Had lunch outside Island Store.

- Reversed route back to Steves Island.

  o Mussels from Steves Island for a seafood feast. (A warning here about Red Tide). Invited Randy and Steve to dinner.

Figure 77 - Map Steves Island to Isle Au Haut

- **Day 3 Steves Island to Crotch Island quarry and Stonington with takeout at Old Quarry Adventures**

  o 6 mile paddle pass by the George Head island sandbar in a whoop-de-doo surfing wave. We visited Crotch Island, once a world renowned

111

granite quarry. We went up the "crotch" past hills of waste chunks of granite. We saw osprey and eagles. We continued along the shoreline of the town of Stonington with its many wharfs of commercial lobster and fishing operations. Lobster boats have the right of way and we learned this quickly as our final hour coincided with lobster boats returning en masse to sell their day's work.

o With expectations of rain and windstorm on Wednesday night, we decided to curtail our trip. After coffee and orange juice, we had a burrito breakfast of pita bread, eggs, cheese and salsa.

o Crotch Island and stone quarry. At the turn of the century, Crotch was one of 33 major island quarries along the Maine coast. They provided work for an estimated 10,000 to 15,000 people, creating a boom-town atmosphere in nearby coastal towns. Crotch Island is an active remnant of what once was a dominant industry and colorful part of Maine's past.

o Crotch Island's 450 acres are littered with the rusted relics of its past, and dotted with hills of waste rock,

Figure 78 - Crotch Island Osprey Nest

chunks of granite that didn't break right and couldn't
be used. A steam-powered Brown hoist crane with a
40-foot boom stands rusting near the V-shaped inlet
that gives Crotch Island its name. We saw an osprey
nest on a hoist crane.

For those interested in more detail:
- **Island fire permits** - There is a telephone number in the
  MITA and hard copy guidebook. There is also a mobile
  phone app http://www.mita.org/app
- **Camp site reservations** -There is no need for camp
  reservations on any of the islands - a MITA member has
  access to all sites on the trail, at any time, unless the guide
  descriptions indicates otherwise)
- **Put-ins available** - The Deer Isle overview page of the
  guide has a list (we selected Old Quarry Ocean Adventures
  http://www.oldquarry.com)

The Maine Island Trail Association (MITA)
The Maine Island Trail Association (http://www.mita.org/) MIT
is a must membership for any outdoor enthusiast considering an
ocean paddle.

As a member of the Maine Island Trail Association (MITA), I enjoy the benefits of an MITA e-newsletter and a MITA Guidebook. Dundee, Cully, Dave and I used this guidebook with its maps and island descriptions to plan our three day 22 mile sea kayak paddle in the Deer Island region of the MIT.

References

- **Ocean Kayaking in the Deer Isle Region of the Maine Coast - Stonington to Isle au Haut** http://outdooradventurers.blogspot.com/2014/07/paddling-deer-isle-region-of-maine.html
- **Sea kayaking and Camping on the Maine Island Trail Outdoor Steve's Blog post of August 2010** http://tiny.cc/u2j44x
- **Deer Isle Region paddle, Bedford Community TV** https://www.youtube.com/watch?v=4FIMlGYn9K0&feature=youtu.be
- **Maine Island Trail Association** http://www.mita.org/
- **Maine Island Trail App** http://www.mita.org/app

Paddling, Hiking & Camping at Connecticut Lakes & Lake Francis

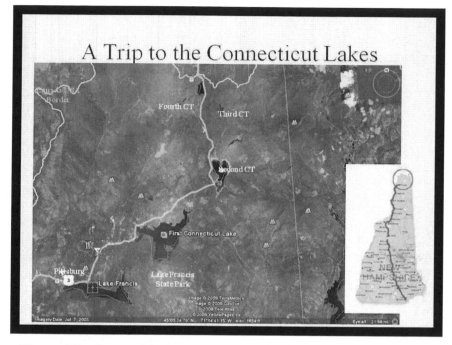

Figure 79 - Route 3 in Red with the Great North Woods circled

Pittsburg, New Hampshire – The Great North Woods

When you say or hear, "Connecticut Lakes and Lake Francis", or "Pittsburg", you are talking about the most northern area of New Hampshire near the Canadian border.

On a Monday in mid-June, John, Dundee, Dick and I drove to the Lake Francis State Park in Pittsburg, NH. Pittsburg has an estimated population of 900 and is the northernmost town in NH and the largest town by area in the state. U.S. Route 3 is the only major highway in the town ending at the Canadian border. Contained within the boundaries of Pittsburg are the Connecticut (CT) Lakes and Lake Francis. These lakes are the headwaters of the 410 mile Connecticut River.

Pittsburg is known for snowmobiling and ATV trails, fishing and hunting, canoeing and kayaking, and its moose. Some of the folks jest, "There are more moose than people."

Pittsburg is an outdoor enthusiast paradise.

Why are we doing this?

1. To visit Moose Alley and almost assure ourselves of seeing moose.

2. We want to straddle the Connecticut River at its 4th Connecticut Lake headwaters outlet.

3. To enjoy my fellow trekkers and The Great North Woods.

4. Because we never want to say, "We wish we had paddled the Connecticut Lakes and Lake Francis."

Great North Woods Itinerary

Here is our schedule for this four-day paddling, hiking and camping trip:

- Monday: Drive to Lake Francis State Park, set up camp, and paddle the lake as daylight permits. The Park will be our camp site for three nights

- Tuesday: Hike to the 4th Connecticut Lake, paddle the 3rd Connecticut Lake, and continue our Lake Francis paddle.

- Wednesday: Paddle 2nd Connecticut Lake, East Inlet and Scott's Bog.

- Thursday: Take down our campsite, paddle 1st Connecticut Lake in the morning, and return home in the afternoon.

The Fourth, Third, Second, First Connecticut Lakes, and Lake Francis flow into each other starting with the tiny Fourth CT Lake on the Canadian border. The water connections are small streams with intermittent sections of white water. Paddling these connections is not really feasible due to the narrowness of the stream, its shallow depth, and obstructing rock formations. For each lake we portage our canoes/kayaks on our car carrier racks.

I used **Google Earth** for maps to orient ourselves and determine distances. **Google** search found the website **Paddling.Net** which had a wonderful article titled, **Connecticut Lakes - Kayak Trip / Canoe Trip.** This article contained a detailed narrative of an earlier trip.

Young's Store was our primary hub for information, food, and adult beverages. "If they do not have it, you do not need it." Next to Young's Store was a wonderful breakfast and lunch café.

The **Buck Rub Pub** is a great place to quench your thirst and have dinner.

They even have their own specially ale - **Buck Rub Brown Ale**!

Figure 80 - Buck Rub Pub

Statistics of Connecticut (CT) Lakes
- 4th CT 78 acres (on the Canadian Border)
- 3rd CT 231 acres (fed by the 4th CT)
- 2nd CT 1,102-acres (fed by the 3rd CT)
- lst CT 3,071 acres (fed by the 2nd CT)
- Lake Francis 1,933 acres (fed by lst CT)

For detail statistics on the Connecticut Lakes go to http://en.wikipedia.org/wiki/Connecticut_Lakes

Pictures are Worth a Thousand Words

Rather than give a narrative of this beautiful area, I will simply show pictures of the areas we visited. At the end of this section I have listed references for more detailed information on The Great North Woods for those outdoor enthusiasts that may want to visit this most beautiful area.

Lake Francis

Figure 81 - Put-in at Lake Francis State Park

Figure 82 - Relaxing at the Campsite

118

Republic of Indian Stream
Did you know that there once was a country between New
Hampshire and Canada? Read on.

- For a few years in the 1830s, an area of today's Pittsburg,
  NH was an independent republic, not part of New
  Hampshire and not part of the United States.
- The US attempted to tax the 360 inhabitants, and Canada
  tried to make them serve in its military, so the people
  decided to establish their own sovereign nation – **The
  Republic of Indian Stream.**
- The existence of the republic was ended by New
  Hampshire in 1835.
- The Webster -Ashburton Treaty of 1842 established the
  border between Canada and the United States.
- Pittsburg is the largest township in the United States,
  covering over 300,000 acres.

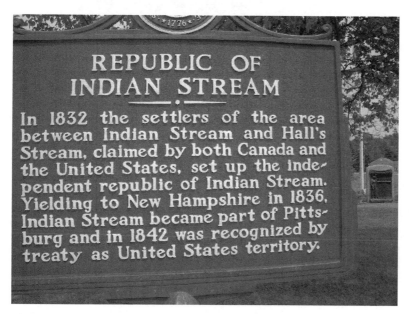

Figure 83 - A Country between the United States and Canada

Fourth Connecticut Lake – Headwaters of the CT River

Figure 84 - A View of the 4th CT Lake

Figure 85 - Steve with one foot on each side of the CT River

Figure 86 - At 4th Connecticut Lake Using the Bug Baffler!

Figure 87 - Straddling the USA and Canada Boundary

Third Connecticut Lake

Figure 88 - Is this 3rd CT Inlet of Water from the 4th CT?

Figure 89 - We Spot a Moose Skeleton on the 3rd CT

First Connecticut Lake

Figure 90 - A Mating Pair of Loons

Figure 91 - Loon Egg on the Man-made Loon Nesting Platform

East Inlet

Figure 92 - Put-in and Take-Out at East Inlet

Figure 93 - Beaver Lodge in East Inlet

18 Mile Moose Alley

I get asked, "What is the best way to see moose in the Great North Woods?" My response is to drive Route 3 (the last 18 miles in NH is nick-named "Moose Alley") and when you spot a stopped car, pull up behind it, as they most likely have spotted moose.

It is safe to say, you will see moose everywhere – including in the middle of the highway – so be careful when driving anywhere in Pittsburg.

"Once you see one, you see them all" is not a valid expression with moose. Each time I see a moose it is a thrill – however, do not get close as these are huge animals. An adult moose can stand close to seven feet high at the shoulder, and males (or "bulls") can weigh as much as 1,500 lbs. Females with a calf are especially dangerous, and during rutting season, a male moose may charge anything. A word to the wise.

Figure 94 - Moose - Scotts Bog from My Canoe

Never say, "I wish I had been to the Great North Woods of New Hampshire"

Video Reference Planning a Paddle to Connecticut Lakes and Lake Francis
- Blog: Paddling the Great North Woods of New Hampshire
  http://outdooradventurers.blogspot.com/2009/04/paddling-and-hiking-connecticut-lakes.html
- Lake Francis State Park
  http://www.nhstateparks.org/explore/state-parks/lake-francis-state-park.aspx
- Buck Rub Pub
  http://www.buckrubpub.com/
- Youngs Store
  http://www.yelp.com/biz/youngs-store-pittsburg
- Connecticut Lakes – Canoe and Kayaks
  http://www.paddling.net/places/showReport.html?450
- Moose
  http://en.wikipedia.org/wiki/Moose#Size_and_weight
- Connecticut Lakes
  http://en.wikipedia.org/wiki/Connecticut_Lakes

Never say, "I wish I had swum across Perkins Pond"

Enjoy a description of seven friends doing a group endurance swim of nearly one mile at Perkins Pond, Sunapee, NH.

The swimmers, accompanied by a safety boat, go across the pond, around a raft, and then return back to the start. The swim takes approximately 40 minutes. The video describes the requirements the athletes must meet before they can swim with the group.

The maps, pictures, and video show snippets of the swim and will give you an "up front and personal" perspective.

The history of this swim started when my 7 and 8 year old boys, Shaun and Tim, asked to drive our 6 horsepower motorboat by themselves. Cathy and I knew the boys could swim, but if an emergency should occur in the boat, we were unconvinced about their ability to swim a long distance to shore.

We told the boys they could only take the boat alone if they could swim across Perkins Pond, and then swim back, all without a life vest. Of course we would accompany them by boat to insure their safety.

Our challenge proved to be an incentive for these young boys to improve and practice their swimming skills. Later that summer they fulfilled their swim agreement, and they were allowed to use the boat, wearing a life vest, by themselves.

Now, with close friends and family, we annually gather to repeat this original challenge – and this time with our grandchildren.

Figure 95 - Swimmers with Lifeguards Carrying Life Vests

Figure 96 - Swimmers & Lifeguards - Annual 1 Mile Swim

Whether as a swimmer or supporter, enjoying the outdoors with friends and family is something you do to never have to say, **"I wish I had swum across Perkins Pond."**

Video Reference Swimming Across Perkins Pond
• **Blog: A Family Swim** http://outdooradventurers.blogspot.com/2010/07/never-say-i-wish-i-had-swum-across.html
• **Video The Swim** http://www.youtube.com/watch?v=6NGRfADxPVU&feature=player_embedded

Kayaking on Cape Cod at the Great Salt Marsh

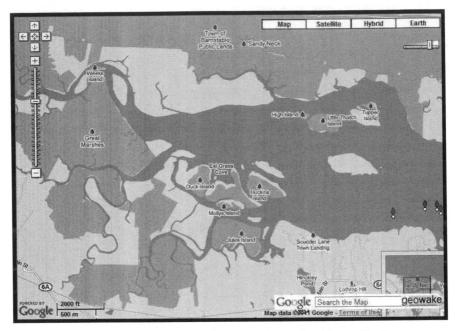

Figure 97 - Map Great Salt Marsh, Cape Cod

- Our friend John invited Dundee, my son Tim, and me for a day's kayak paddle near John's Cape Cod home. We expected an easy paddle in Barnstable Harbor's protected waters.

  The 11 AM put-in at Scudder Lane's paved ramp began an hour before low tide. Due to winds of 10 to 15 miles per hour, mixed with the change to incoming tide, we experienced choppy water and one to two-foot waves -- and a somewhat exciting paddle.

  We had light winds as we crossed the harbor to Sandy Neck and paddled along its beautiful sand beach. We saw the power of the ocean on the great salt marsh as you will see in the below video of chunks of sand being pulled into the bay.

130

Figure 98 - Lunch Sandy Neck

- We walked on Sandy Neck beach – and this required pulling our kayaks over low tide sand bars.

- We did not paddle the extreme marshes as low tide left only mud lanes like quick sand. Our brief venture into the marsh required stepping ashore and going through one to two foot-deep mud to get to the high water grass. My water sandals were nearly lost as the sucking mud would only release my feet after I removed my sandals.

- When the tide changed, we experienced tidal phenomena at spots where low water sand bars and deep water met. You will see in this brief video water frothing, similar to white water flowing over rocks – but rocks were not present. Indeed I was at first hesitant to cross this very real white line, but after passing through a few of these areas I realized the froth was only the outgoing and incoming water meeting on the low tide turn.

- We paddled by oyster farmers "up close and personal" as

they cultivated their oyster beds.

- Our water tour of Barnstable Harbor and its Great Salt Marsh lasted four and a half hours.

Directions:

"Barnstable Harbor is located on Cape Cod Bay between the barrier beach of Sandy Neck and an extensive saltmarsh estuary between Sandwich and the Cape Cod Canal to the northeast and Wellfleet to the southeast. It's roughly nine nautical miles from the entrance of the Cape Cod Canal to Barnstable Harbor.

Figure 99 - Low Tide at Barnstable Harbor

It's important to note the tide and weather conditions. If it's particularly nasty, you may not want to go because of the Barnstable Harbor entrance being shallow water and the east-west tidal currents that shift north to south in the harbor channel. A tidal range of nearly 10 feet makes the harbor prone to shoaling and sandbars. It is best to enter the harbor on a rising tide. Once in the harbor channel, stay well within the markers, as the areas off Beach Point and Sandy Neck Light are very shallow and prone to strong currents.

Figure 100 - Three Amigos Kayaking

Nearby Scudder Lane has a paved ramp that launches into the harbor, but it has limited parking. Finally, while boaters would be wise to avoid Barnstable Harbor's tricky network of creeks and marshland, kayakers and paddlers will love it. However, if embarking on an unguided trek, be sure to take along a GPS and/or a cell phone, as it's easy to become stranded or lost in the Great Marshes' maze of creeks. Use NOAA chart 13251."

I never have to say, "I wish I had kayaked the Great Salt Marsh of Cape Cod"

Figure 101 - Yes, there are Turkeys on Cape Cod

Read more at:
- http://www.trails.com/tcatalog_trail.aspx?trailid=CGN029-026
- http://www.greatmarshkayaktours.com/naturalists_dream_tour.htm

---

Video References Kayaking on Cape Cod
- Blog: Kayaking on Cape Cod at the Great Salt Marsh
  http://outdooradventurers.blogspot.com/2011/06/kayaking-in-barnstable-harbor-and-great.html
- Kayaking at Cape Cod's Great Salt Marsh
  http://www.youtube.com/watch?v=4x8vx6J8Kzk&feature=player_embedded

Camp OutdoorSteve Training Youth in Canoe Rescue

An afternoon learning canoe rescue and self-confidence.

My teenager grandson was visiting our camp in Sunapee, NH. We were sitting around a campfire with his Sunapee friends. In the course of our campsite storytelling, I shared with them my experience participating in a canoe rescue on one of my paddling trips to the Allagash Wilderness Waterway in Maine.

The message I wanted to convey to these youths was, "practice makes perfect."

Briefly, on a canoe trip to the 34 mile Moose River Bow Trip, two of our group flipped their canoe in the middle of Holeb Pond. My friend John and I were nearby, and we quickly paddled over, tied a rope to the overturned canoe, and towed them to shore – an exhausting paddle that took nearly a half hour. My cousin Linwood, a Master Maine Guide, asked, "Why did you not rescue them?" My response was, "We did!"

Linwood then proceeded to tell us we should have righted the swamped canoe in the middle of the lake draining it of water, then getting the two paddlers back in the boat, and letting them paddle themselves back to shore. No need for an exhausting paddle towing an overturned canoe with two bodies hanging on.

At our next campsite Linwood would teach us how to do this. The next day for nearly four hours, myself and six companions, under the tutelage of Linwood, learned and practiced two types of canoe rescue scenarios:

1) **Two or more canoes are paddling together and one flips over**. An upright canoe assists the capsized canoers by righting their boat, emptying it of water, retrieving their gear, and standing by while they re-enter their boat (even in deep water)
2) **Two paddlers, alone, flip their canoe and need to upright it without outside help**.

Interestingly - and here was my message to the youths about "practice makes perfect" - the next year myself with the same group of friends were paddling across Eagle Lake on the Allagash Wilderness Waterway. Suddenly, one of our canoes capsized in the middle of the one-mile wide lake.

By the time we reached them, the two occupants were swimming holding onto the canoe with their tents, food, and other camping gear drifting nearby (all protected by dry bags). With hardly a word said, this group, who had practiced the canoe rescue the prior year, immediately began their learned "two or more canoers paddling together" rescue technique. Within minutes, both paddlers were back in their righted and dry canoe with their gear intact, and we continued on to our next campsite.

The message to the youths is "practice makes perfect."

Camp OutdoorSteve Teaching "Practice Makes Perfect" Canoe Rescues

The next day after this fireside chat of our true rescue, my grandson and his friends asked if they could learn the canoe rescue. The below sequence of pictures and the following video is a wonderful afternoon of fun and learning. Most importantly, it demonstrated the value of practice and the resulting self-confidence if one day they face what might be a real canoe rescue situation.

Figure 102 - The Flip!

Figure 103 - Emptying the Canoe of Water

The two paddlers in the water get on one end of the overturned canoe and push down until the other end of the canoe releases its vacuum and rises out of the water. The canoe is then pulled onto the rescue boat and slid perpendicular across to its midpoint, resulting in no water in the canoe.

Figure 104 - Canoe Turned Over and Slid back into the Water

Figure 105 - Dry Canoe is brought parallel to rescue boat, braced by Rescuers, and the swimmers climb back in from the side.

Figure 106 - Away They Go!

Practice – Practice – Practice – Then the Actual Rescue is Easy.

Video Reference Practicing the Canoe Rescue at Perkins Pond
http://youtu.be/gRFsWovoQ3g

Vermont Wilderness camping and paddling

"Everyone must do something. I believe I will go outdoors with
family and friends."

Figure 107 - Super Swimming in an outdoors environment

In early July I did two days of paddling and one night of tenting in
the Green River Reservoir of northern Vermont. My companions
were my adult son Tim; my two teenage grandchildren; my friend
Dundee and his adult son Paul; and Paul's two teenage boys and
his ten year old daughter. Our transportation was three kayaks and
three canoes.

The 5 minute video is better than words, but here is a summary:

- I used the Green River Reservoir web site to identify our
  preferred camp site and make reservations.

- The nine of us in three cars had a two plus hour trip from Sunapee, NH

- Access to the Green River Reservoir is only through the Park Ranger Station

- All camp sites are only accessed via the water

- We had a half hour paddle to our chosen camp site #25

- We had intermittent rain throughout the first day, BUT rain in no way hindered our wonderful family and friends trip.

- Paul was our top notch menu planner and Chef as he did on a prior trip (Paddling the Waters of Quetico Provincial Park in Ontario, Canada). Paul made a marvelous macaroni, cheese, and hot dog supper – and a great McNestler egg-cheese-bacon-English muffin breakfast.

- We had three tents and a large camp tarp on site #25.

- We decided to see if we could start a fire with flint and steel – and each of us took a turn at this task. You will see this teaching moment in the videos.

Figure 108 - Flint and Steel Start our Dinner Fire

- This is a magnificent lake to swim in clear and deep water.
  The surrounding cliffs drop away into eight plus feet of
  water with no shoreline – so a person really must be a
  swimmer to dive and swim to shore. All nine of us are
  experienced swimmers.

- NEVER jump into water without first checking for rocks,
  depths and dangerous obstacles. See the video for our cliff
  jumping fun.

- In the evening we went for a paddle around Big Island (we
  had stayed on site #33 in 2012 Peak Foliage Paddling and
  Camping in the Green River Reservoir of Northern
  Vermont)

Figure 109 - Cliff Jumping

- Wildlife is prominent in this area. We saw nesting loons, herons, beaver signs, and even moose scat. We were told eagles were there, but we saw none.

No grandfather, father, or friend could have enjoyed a better time. Life is great!

For those interested in more details of our trip see a 25 minute video titled **Wilderness camping and paddling with family and friends: Green River Reservoir** (http://youtu.be/joTKzJI1r90).

About Green River Reservoir
Green River Reservoir became a state park in March 1999 when 5110 acres were purchased from the Morrisville Water and Light Department. This is not your typical Vermont State Park – Green River Reservoir provides camping and paddling experiences in a remote setting. All campsites can only be reached by paddling to them - some are a 1 to 2-mile paddle from the launch site.

The park will remain in its wild and undeveloped condition, with low-impact, compatible recreational use allowed on and around the Reservoir. Management activities will be only those necessary to maintain the property's character, protect the environment and critical resources, demonstrate sustainable forest and wildlife management, control excessive recreational use, and ensure high-quality outdoor experiences for visitors.

The 653-acre Reservoir includes about 19 miles of shoreline, one of the longest stretches of undeveloped shorelines in Vermont. Access to the park is in the southern part of the Reservoir off of Green River Dam Road. The Reservoir is designated as a "quiet" lake under Vermont "Use of Public Waters Rules." Boats powered by electric motors up to 5 mph and human-powered watercraft (canoes, kayaks, etc.) are allowed.

There are 28 remote campsites at various locations around the Reservoir. Camping is allowed only at designated campsites and can only be reached by boat. Each remote site has a maximum site occupancy based on the characteristics of the site. There is one designated group campsite that can accommodate up to 12 people. Some campsites are closed each season and rehabilitated due to overuse through the years.

References
- **Green River Reservoir**
  http://www.vtstateparks.com/htm/grriver.htm
- Paddling the Waters of Quetico Provincial Park in Ontario, Canada http://tiny.cc/sfv26x
- Peak Foliage Paddling and Camping in the Green River Reservoir of Northern Vermont http://tiny.cc/xgv26x

Figure 110 - Fun for all ages Green River Reservoir, Vermont

Looking into the eye of a Rainbow

At 7 pm on Wednesday July 9, 2014 I witnessed a magnificent double rainbow and its complete reflection on the water. In essence, *"I looked into the Eye of a Rainbow"*.

Figure 111 - A double rainbow over Perkins Pond

Figure 112 - "Eye of the rainbow" with *Isle of View* at center

Look closely at the above picture. In the very middle of this "Rainbow Eye" you will see Nestler's Island in Perkins Pond. This picture is indeed a "one in a trillion" shot. (Photo by Dundee).

Perkins Pond is a 157 acre pond located in the Dartmouth-Sunapee Region of New Hampshire.

References
- **Video and Blog**: Looking into the Eye of a Rainbow http://outdooradventurers.blogspot.com/2014/07/i-looked-into-eye-of-rainbow.html

Paddling the Northern Forest Canoe Trail Section 6: The Clyde River - Island Pond to Pensioner Pond

Three friends and I spent four days paddling the Clyde and Nulhegan Rivers and Spectacle Pond – parts of what the NFCT calls section 6. Island Pond is the highest point in the NFCT, and it serves as the headwaters for the Clyde River, which flows 40 miles northwest to Lake Memphremagog and leads to the Saint Lawrence River.Island Pond, through Spectacle Pond, is also the headwaters for the Nulhegan River, which flows east to the Connecticut River.

The referenced blog and video will focus on the Clyde River.

Figure 113 - Section 6 Clyde River

We tented at Brighton State Park at Spectacle Pond shoreline for four days.

Figure 114 - Campsite at Brighton State Park, Spectacle Pond

Water Conditions

- On Day One the Clyde River water was clear and moving slowly from our Island Pond put-in to Ten Mile Square Road take-out. Paddling from Island Pond to Five Mile Square Road was five miles of zigzagging and took us about four hours. We overcame many obstacles such as downed trees in the river, beaver dams, Class I-II boulder fields from a washed out logging-era dam, and walls of wood debris and blow-downs. The water level exposed many of the felled trees and was a challenge to our kayak and canoeing skills to overcome these barriers without portaging. The width of the river from Island Pond to Ten Mile Square Road was narrow (ten to twenty feet wide).

- Day Two was an all-day drenching, soaking rainstorm, and we only managed a brief evening paddle on beautiful Spectacle Pond passing the NFCT sign to portage to the Nulhegan River.

149

- On Day Three we continued from our Ten Mile Square Road take-out nine miles to Pensioner Pond. Certainly the previous day's deluge had an impact on the Clyde's width and speed which overflows with high water levels. We estimated a 3 to 4 mph current that really moved us along. This Day Three section had more marsh and fewer trees than Day One from Island Pond to Ten Mile Square.

Places to get answers for questions on conditions on the Clyde:

- We used the highly recommended NFCT online **Trip Planner** (http://www.northernforestcanoetrail.org/tripplanner/) to plan and map our trip. We also purchased the **NFCT Lake Memphremagog to Connecticut River Section 6** water protected map - and referred to it frequently throughout our paddle.

- The **Island Pond to Upper Clyde** reference has a very good **Trip Summary** of paddling miles and times. (http://www.northernforestcanoetrail.org/media/Island_Pond_And_The_Upper_Clyde.pdf). Get answers to such questions as "How long does it take to paddle from Island Pond to Five Mile Square Road, and then to Ten Mile Square Road? How long does it take to paddle from Ten Mile Square Road to Pensioner Pond?"

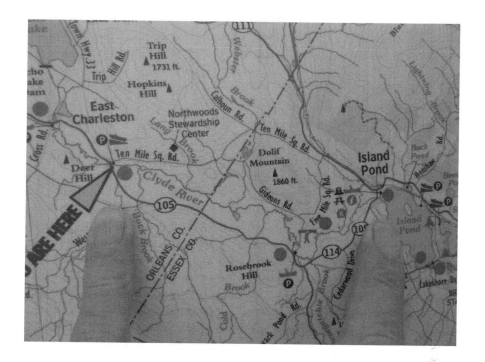

Figure 115 - Map of Island Pond to Ten Mile Square Road

Want to know what it feels like to paddle the Clyde River? What does the countryside look like? What obstacles may be encountered? Want to see Tim, John and Dundee paddle a short section of Class I – II boulder field rapids?

Before you watch the below video let me get you psyched for watching my friends go through the rapids.

Normally, as we approach log dams and other obstacles in the river, we slow and check the area for our approach, and then go through one person at a time, waiting to make sure each person safely gets through before the next person goes. When we know rapids are ahead, we stop before the rapids and scout the best way to go through the rapids.

About four miles from our put-in at Island Pond, I was the first person through one of the many fallen trees blocking the river, and my intent was to paddle clear of this obstacle and wait for my fellow paddlers. However the fallen tree was on a bend, and when I made it through the barrier on the bend I immediately found myself upon what looked like Class II white water without a place to pull out and wait for the next paddler.

Essentially I was committed to these rapids with boulders and small drops, not really knowing how rough they were nor how long they would last. I was safely able to make it through this two hundred yard set of rapids – and as you will see next, my friends did like-wise. Enjoy the short movie clip made when I ran back on the riverbank, too late to warn my friends of their upcoming surprise.

Clicking the below video reference shares my excitement filming my friends negotiating rapids.

Figure 116 - Our white water paddlers

So what is the Northern Forest Canoe Trail (NFCT)?
The NFCT is a living reminder of when rivers were both highways
and routes of communications; the Trail is a celebration of the
Northern Forest. The Trail is 740 miles of historic waterway
traveled by Native Americans. It begins/ends in Fort Kent Maine,
and travels through Maine, New Hampshire, Vermont, Quebec,
and ending/beginning in Old Forge, New
York. http://www.northernforestcanoetrail.org.

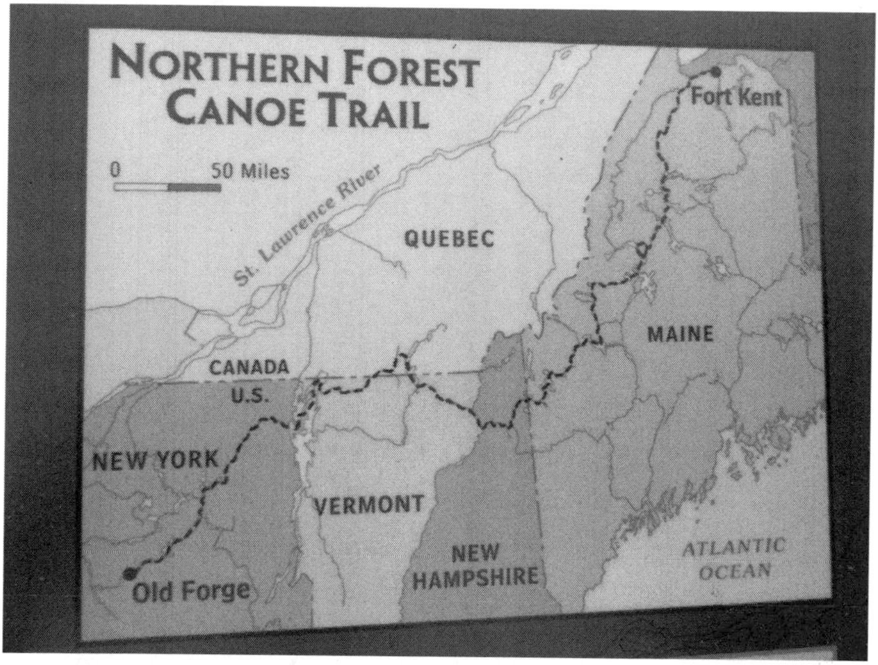

Figure 117 - Map of Northern Forest Canoe Trail

The NFCT is a journey through the landscape of the
northeast. The land speaks of its history – of rocks and ruins,
people and plants, and natural and economic forces at play.
The sections of the NFCT that friends and I have paddled are:

- The Allagash Wilderness Waterway

- Lake Umbagog; Androscoggin River

- Lake Memphremagog

153

- Connecticut River

- Moose River and Attean Pond on the historic "Moose River Bow Trip"

- Umbazooksus Stream

- Clyde River, Nulhegan River, and Spectacle Pond

- Four Days in Northern New Hampshire with Family and Friends Hiking, Paddling, Tenting and Moose Sighting.http://outdooradventurers.blogspot.com/2012/07/four-days-in-new-hampshire-of-family.html

- Exploring Lake Umbagog – a Gem in the Great North Woods http://outdooradventurers.blogspot.com/2010/09/exploring-lake-umbagog-gem-in-great.html

- Paddling the Allagash Wilderness Waterway http://outdooradventurers.blogspot.com/2009/07/paddling-allagash-wilderness-waterway.html

Special 24 Minute Clyde River Video: Clicking http://tiny.cc/ze954x presents the Northern Forest Canoe Trail ordeal of a writer/cameraman who is occupied as a kayaker on the Clyde River in the Northeast Kingdom of Vermont.

References
Video and Blog: **Paddling the Northern Forest Canoe Trail Section 6: The Clyde River - Island Pond to Pensioner Pond** http://outdooradventurers.blogspot.com/2013/06/paddling-northern-forest-canoe-trail.html

- Northern Forest Canoe Trail http://www.northernforestcanoetrail.org

- Island Pond and the Upper Clyde http://www.northernforestcanoetrail.org/media/Island_Pond_And_The_Upper_Clyde.pdf

- NFCT online Trip Planner http://www.northernforestcanoetrail.org/tripplanner/

- OutdoorSteve.com
  http://www.outdoorsteve.com

- Blog: Outdoor Enthusiast
  http://outdooradventurers.blogspot.com/

- Paddling the Northern Forest Canoe Trail: The Clyde River from Island Pond to Ten Mile Square
  http://youtu.be/ZF6KswIEPHM

- Brighton State Park, Vermont
  http://www.vtstateparks.com/htm/brighton.htm

Paddling the Northern Forest Canoe Trail Section 2: Long Lake to Village of Saranac Lake

Welcome to the **Northern Forest Canoe Trail**. The NFCT is a living reminder of when rivers were both highways and routes of communications. The Trail is 740 miles of historic waterway traveled by Native Americans. Its west to east direction begins in Old Forge, New York, and travels through Vermont, Quebec, New Hampshire and ends in Fort Kent Maine. The non-profit that established the Trail divides the trail into 13 sections and offers detailed maps for each of these sections.

Figure 118 - Take-out at Village of Saranac Lake

Our journey was Section 2 in the Adirondack and Saranac region of northern New York. We began at the Long Lake bridge paddling in a north-east direction and ended 42 miles and 3 ½ days later at the Village of Saranac.

We hired Adirondack Lakes & Trails Outfitters to drive us to the put-in so we could leave both our vehicles at the Flower Lake take-out – thus saving ourselves 2 plus hours when we were homeward bound.

Our trip included transfers through two hand-operated locks to convey paddlers between waterways, and three very demanding portages totaling 11.5 plus miles.

Our 3 ½ day itinerary:

- Day 1: A 15 plus mile paddle on Long Lake, then a 1.6 mile portage around Raquette falls – which took three trips totaling 4.8 miles - with our day ending at the Palmer Brook lean-to on the Raquette River.

- Day 2: Raquette River to Stony Creek Ponds, a 1.1 mile Indian Carry portage - which took five trips totaling 5.5 miles – followed by the .4 mile Bartlett Carry into Middle Saranac Lake to our campsite on Norway Island. A twelve miles paddling day.

- Day 3: We paddled through the Upper Locks into Lower Saranac Lake to our campsite on Partridge Island. About an 8 mile paddling day.

- Day 4: Lower Saranac Lake to First Pond into Second Pond and through the Lower Locks of the Saranac River into Oseetah Lake, and then into Lake Flower for our final take-out at the Village of Saranac Lake. An 8 mile paddling day

This Section 2 water highway has no fresh drinking water sources. Dehydration can be a major issue. We restocked our drinking water at night boiling lake water with our Jet Boil. In addition, it rained our second night, and we directed rainwater from our camp tarp to our cooking pans hence to our water bottles – thus saving Jet Boil fuel.

Figure 119 - Passing through the Locks of NFCT Section 2
More specifics of our Section 2 paddle, portages, and locks can be found in a day-by-day 50 minute web link video at Bedford Community TV **http://tiny.cc/ydb64x**.

Day 2 – Palmer Brook Lean-to to Norway Island, Middle Saranac Lake

We arose in our Palmer Brook lean-to campsite with the smell of fresh coffee. Dundee was up early. John followed asking "How do you want your eggs and bacon?"

Gary, a Park Ranger, visited our camp and emphasized issues of dehydration, particularly on the two upcoming portages at Indian Carry (1.1 miles) and Bartlett carry (.4 miles). He advised us on maps of Section 2, and reminded us to be sure our campfire was completely out before we left camp.

Given our first day had a very demanding 1.6 mile portage that we had to do three times for 4.8 miles (carry canoe, return to take-out, carry backpacks), we decided at Indian Carry the four of us would carry one canoe. This proved to be really exhausting, as we did five trips over the 1.1 Indian Carry trail (carry the 65 lb old town, walk back, carry the 72 lb Grumman canoe, walk back, and carry the backpacks). These five trips totaled 5.5 miles.

Throughout our portages we continually drank water every ten minutes or so to prevent dehydration. Even so, we were exhausted by the time all our canoes and gear were at the Upper Saranac Lake put-in.

Indian Carry revealed a very moving token of New York hospitality. As we were lugging the 65 lb Old Town, and we were really exhausted with at least another half mile to reach the Upper Saranac put-in, a fellow waved as he went by us in his truck. Lo and behold he backed up, rolled down his window, and asked, "Do you want to put those canoes in my truck?"

Brian, you are an angel!! He saved us at least an hour of portaging – and certainly provided the physical relief we needed. I gave Brian my OutdoorSteve business card, and told him to send me an email so I could mail him a signed copy of **Outdoor Play: Fun 4 4 Seasons**.

We paddled on the Upper Saranac for an hour and came to Bartlett's Carry. We were now sharing our two bottles of remaining fresh water – like in rationing. And we had the Bartlett .4 mile carry left for at least 1.2 miles, AND if we had four people for each canoe, we had nearly two miles left! After our grueling human transport of 5.5 miles at Indian Carry (due to four of us per canoe), our exhaustion told us to return to two people per canoe to eliminate an extra one mile portage.

We finished Bartlett Carry still alive and entered Middle Saranac Lake. It was about an hour's paddle to Norway Island, our campsite for the night. Amen!!

Our Norway Island campsite (#74) was perfect. It was the only campsite on the island and had pine trees growing amongst the rocks.

The ranger at Palmer Brook told us about a coming storm that evening, so we immediately put up our tents, and then a tarp over the campsite table. Indeed that evening we had a terrible rain storm with lightning and wind. Once the camp was set up, Dundee took a Middle Saranac Lake cool, clear water swim. The rest of us were too exhausted.

I dreamed about our canoes being washed away, paddles gone, and tarp down. I was too exhausted to get out of my tent. My fears were for naught as in the morning the site was calm and everything was in its rightful place.

Day 3 We paddle today from our Norway Island campsite on Middle Sarnanc Lake to a Partridge Island campsite in Lower Saranac Lake
We started our day with another great breakfast by Chef John. We appreciated John's menu planning, food acquisition, and certainly his meals were fit for royalty.

Similar to our prior two days, we have been abused by mosquitos, black flies and whatever flying bugs we meet on our trip. I am not a DEET person and had been wearing a long sleeve jersey as well as a full body netting. One section we paddled before the locks, turned into a serious humming sound – and by that I mean bug sounds at a high and steady pitch. It was like we were immersed in a swarm of vibrating insects. What a surreal experience.

Today would be the self-operated Uppers Lock from Middle Sarnanc Lake to Lower Sarnanc. Enjoy our first lock transition as we thoroughly appreciated the experience of going from a higher lake to a lower lake – bypassing a severe set of rapids.

After passing through the Upper Lock, we paddled another hour to our campsite for the night on Partridge Island. It was my turn to go swimming in this beautiful clear Lower Saranac Lake.

As you will see in the 50 minute video link on Bedford Community TV **http://tiny.cc/ydb64x** we were more relaxed on Day 3 as we had our strength back with no portages and plenty of potable water. Our relaxation time included:

- Starting our campfire with sparks

- Sharing how we eat our pudding without a spoon when on our camping trips.

- Learning to tie quick release knots for putting up and taking down our tarp

- Walked to ledges on the island to view the beautiful sunset.

Day 4 – Our last day on Section 2 of the NFCT in the Adirondacks and Saranac. We paddled from our Partridge Island campsite through a second hand-operated lock to Oseetah Lake and then to our take-out at the Village of Saranac on the north end of Flower Lake.

We estimated Partridge Island to be about 8 miles or 3 hours of paddling to our take-out at the north end of Flower Lake.

Yesterday, when we passed through the Upper locks, I was in the canoe being lowered. Today was Tim's turn to experience this unique procedure transiting the Lower Lock, that feeling of our canoes and gear being transported via water from Lower Saranac Lake to Oseetah Lake.

No lock operator was present at the lock and Dundee operated the manual controls while John and Tim paddled into the locks – and I documented their transition with videos. The whole descent would take about 30 minutes – mostly waiting for the lock to fill – and then empty and gently hand our canoes and gear, and us, into lower Oseetah lake.

The paddling was easy and we soaked in the wilderness and beauty of the Adirondacks. We saw deer, huge rock formations, and shared highlights of our Saranac paddle. We all agreed, the portaging of our 65 lb and 72 lb canoes was the toughest part of the trip. On our next trip requiring extensive portages, we definitely would rent 40 lb canoes.

After we finished at the Village take-out, we went to the NFCT Kiosk and signed the NFCT log book.

Never say, "I wish I had paddled the **Northern Forest Canoe Trail Section 2** in the Adirondack and Saranac wilderness."

References

Video and Blog: Paddling the Northern Forest Canoe Trail Section 2: Long Lake to Village of Saranac Lake
http://outdooradventurers.blogspot.com/2014/06/paddling-northern-forest-canoe-trail.html

Adirondack Lakes & Trails Outfitters

http://www.adirondackoutfitters.com/

Adirondack State Park

https://en.wikipedia.org/wiki/Adirondack_Park

How long does it take to boil drinking water?

http://modernsurvivalblog.com/health/how-long-to-boil-drinking-water/

Northern Forest Canoe Trail

http://www.northernforestcanoetrail.org/

OutdoorSteve.com

http://www.outdoorsteve.com

Figure 120 - Overview of NFCT Section 2 Trip

Carson in Warrior Dash - Mountain City, GA

See a five minute video of a race Carson did on a Saturday in Mountain City, Georgia. The Warrior Dash is the world's largest obstacle race series, held on the most rugged terrain in more than 50 locations across the globe. Participants tackle a fierce 3-4 mile course and 12 extreme obstacles.

Figure 120 - Rope Climb

Figure 121 - Ready for final climb of nets

Figure 122 - Sliding into the mud bath and the finish

Figure 123 - Carson and his support team

References

- **Video and Blog: Carson in Warrior Dash- Mountain City, GA**
  http://outdooradventurers.blogspot.com/2014/04/carson-in-warrior-dash-mountain-city-ga.html
- To learn more about the Warrior Dash go to http://www.warriordash.com.

Hula Hoop Training in Live Oak, Florida

Figure 124 - Hula Hoop at Live Oak, Florida

Figure 125 - And the Winner is!

References

- **Video and Blog:** Hula Hoop Training in Live Oak, FL
  http://tiny.cc/5nbg6x

New London Triathlon - Family of Three Generations

My adult son Shaun and I are fellow triathletes. Is it possible we could get my grandson Carson in the same triathlon?

Teenage friends of my thirteen year-old grandson, Carson, asked me if he might be interested in being a teammate on a triathlon team they were putting together. They wanted Carson to do the ¼ mile swim leg – the initial leg of the swim-bike-run triathlon.

A telephone call to my son Shaun asking if my grandson might be interested had a response of "Ask Carson".

A follow-up text message from Carson, met with a one word response, "Yes!"

Carson's positive reply peaked my interest in being in the same race, so I registered, as Shaun did, as an individual entry to do all three legs.

Two weeks before the race, I experienced a hamstring injury. While I could swim and bike with this injury, I knew I could not complete a 3.1 mile run.

Hmm, maybe since Carson was starting the first leg for his team, I might ask Carson to do my third leg – the run? Would the race officials allow this? Would the officials allow me to change my registration from an individual entry to a team entry?

I contacted the person responsible for the race registration; I explained my injury situation; asked if I could change from an individual entry to a team entry; and asked if my grandson, Carson, who was already registered on another team for the first leg, could do my third leg - the run. Her response was a very affirmative "YES!" to all my questions and concerns (I did need to increase my registration fee as the team fee is higher than an individual entry).

	Perkins Pond Team	**The Priests**	**Shaun**
Swim	Carson	Steve	Shaun
Bike	Christian	Steve	Shaun
Run	Nicholas	Carson	Shaun

The above chart shows my grandson and I start the race as competitors in the swim, and finish as teammates with his run. Fantastic!

Figure 126 - Teammates and competitors – and then friends

Figure 127 - Three Generations and Friends – all finishers

Enjoy the below four minute video as three generations of the Priest family enjoy the New London New Hampshire Triathlon.

Reference
- Video and Blog: New London New Hampshire Triathlon - a Family Affair for Three Generations http://outdooradventurers.blogspot.com/2013/08/new-london-new-hampshire-triathlon.html

Never say, "I wish I had been on the Mount Sunapee Zip Line Canopy Tour"

A Visit with Family to Mount Sunapee

My sixteen year old granddaughter, Madison, thirteen year old grandson, Carson, son Tim, and grandmother (Wife) Cathy, saw the below video of Sarah and I on the Mount Sunapee Canopy Zip Line Tour, and expressed their desire to never say, **"I wish I had been on the Mt Sunapee Canopy Zip Line."** A week later all four achieved their wish.

Figure 128 - Ready for the eight station zip line tour

What is a zip line? Well, a zip line (also known as a zip wire, aerial runway, aerial rope slide, death slide, flying fox, or canopy tour) consists of a pulley suspended on a cable, usually made of stainless steel, mounted on an incline. It is designed to enable a user propelled by gravity to travel from the top to the bottom of the inclined cable by holding onto, or attaching to, the freely moving pulley. (https://en.wikipedia.org/wiki/Zip-line).

The Mount Sunapee Canopy Zip-Line Tour features a series of zip lines, rope bridges and rappelling as you descend from the top of Mt Sunapee's South Peak. There are **eight zip lines** in total highlighted by the **final leap on 1,000' dual zip lines which end on a platform behind the Welcome Center**, from where we rappelled back down to earth. From the first tree platform to the last platform we traveled a total distance of almost ¾ mile as we flew above the forest floor. Groups of no more than eight people are led by two guides as you fly through a canopy of oak, beech, maple, birch and evergreen trees. There are six ski trail crossings that offer spectacular views of the surrounding mountains and Lake Sunapee.
[http://www.mountsunapee.com/mtsunapeewinter/index.asp]

Click the Below Video and Go on Our Zip Line Tour

See Sarah and Steve on Their Zip Line Tour

My wife and I had visitors from Georgia. Sarah, their sixteen year old daughter, heard about the Mount Sunapee Canopy Zip Line Tour. Sarah, being a fellow outdoor enthusiast, wanted to do the Zip Line Tour – and so did I.

Sarah and I were the only people in our group, and our tour took less than two hours.

To qualify for admittance to the zip line tour, you must be 10 years old or older and between 80 and 260 pounds.

We had two excellent guides, Mary and Martha. They absolutely were part of the positive experience of doing this adventure – and they ensured our safety.

Figure 129 - Safety is always first

- **The Clip-In** At each platform, the moment we reached the platform we were clipped to the tree – not once but two times. We could not fall off the platform if we slipped, stumbled, or were pushed. As Sarah and I took turns jumping first, we remained clipped to the tree until we were positioned, and one by one – a clip was release and then re-clipped to the zip line. Thus, again, in case we jumped or slipped before being ready or instructed, we still would not fall from the platform.

- Before each jump, we received instructions pertinent to that particular zip line, bridge, or belay we were about to do. [Belaying refers to a variety of techniques climbers use to exert tension on a climbing rope so that a falling climber does not fall very far. A climbing partner typically applies friction at the other end of the rope whenever the climber is not moving, and removing the friction from the rope whenever the climber needs more rope to continue climbing. The term "belay" also means the place where the belayer is anchored; this is typically a ledge, but may be a hanging belay, where the belayer is suspended from the rock, or in our case the wooden platform [http://en.wikipedia.org/wiki/Belaying].

- Before each of the eight leaps, Mary or Martha would explain what to do, and then the guide would go first with her leap – this served both to demonstrate proper departure and to have the guide at the end of the zip line to assist your landing if necessary.

  The guide at the beginning of the zip line would wait for the guide at the other end to yell "Clear", and then confirm it with a "clear" – and then I/Sarah would jump.

The First Leap
We rode the Sunapee Ski lift to South Peak to our first platform. We then climbed about fifteen feet on a rope ladder up the hillside platform. Now came the moment I was there for – the zip line leap.

I must confess my stomach was tight for this first jump – and I was sweating with nervousness and anxious anticipation. I looked downhill at the next platform hundreds of feet away, and thought, "What am I doing here?" I had all kinds of reservations as to whether I truly wanted to jump from this height. Would the harness hold me? Was I strong enough to hold on to the harness strap (no worry here as the harness cable strap was simply to give me "confidence.")

My first jump was here. I was clicked to the cable, and Martha said, "OK Steve, you can jump." I looked at Martha to be doubly positive I heard her correctly, and asked, "Is it OK to jump?" [It never hurts to be absolutely certainly about this.]

Figure 130 - Sarah takes the leap of faith

You have to believe in the equipment and in your guides!! The adrenaline rush came and the commitment was there. I leaped!!! The harness held and I was flying down the cable with an eagle's view of Mount Sunapee and Lake Sunapee. It was a thrill!!

The Leap of Trust
With each zip line jump I gained confidence in myself. As I readied for the fourth zip line leap, Mary asked, "Do you want to try the *Leap of Trust?*" I questioned her as to what she meant, and she said, "You jump off backwards without holding on to the harness strap. Watch me demonstrate." She took a short run off the platform and jumped backwards into the open sky!

You will need to watch the below video to see if I made the Leap of Trust.

Figure 131 - Steve comes in for a platform landing

How to Dress

The Zip Line tour operates rain or shine, so you must dress appropriately. They recommend hiking boots or sneakers, and no open-toed shoes, sandals, or other footwear that can fall off. Sarah and I both wore sneakers - and this was perfect for us in warm summer weather.

In the summer it is suggested that participants wear shorts that fall mid-thigh or lower and either short or long sleeves. No tank tops are allowed as the harness straps may cause discomfort. They provided all needed safety equipment including a helmet and zip line harness. You may also want to bring sunscreen, bug repellent, a small pack or fanny pack for cameras, snacks, etc.

You need to watch the below video to see Sarahs and my first leap, our "Leap of Trust", rope bridge crossing and belaying.

Figure 132 - Guides and participants

To see the web site for the Mount Sunapee Canopy Tour go to http://www.mountsunapee.com/mtsunapeewinter/adventurepark/welcome.asp

To see an 11 minute video on our Mount Sunapee Canopy Zip Line Tour http://tiny.cc/0f4t6x for the unedited thrills of the Zip Line.

References
- **Video and Blog: Never say, "I wish I had been on the Mount Sunapee Zip Line Canopy Tour"** http://outdooradventurers.blogspot.com/2013/07/never-say-i-wish-i-had-been-on-mount.html

Fall

The roads are lovely, dark, and deep. But I have promises to keep, and miles to go before I sleep, and miles to go before I sleep. – Robert Frost

McDaniel's Marsh Wildlife Management Area

Two friends and I picked a cloudy day in early November to kayak McDaniel's Marsh in Springfield, New Hampshire. We put-in at 9 am and took-out around noon. Indeed, there is a diversity of wildlife at McDaniel's Marsh.

Figure 133 - Kayakers at McDaniel's Marsh

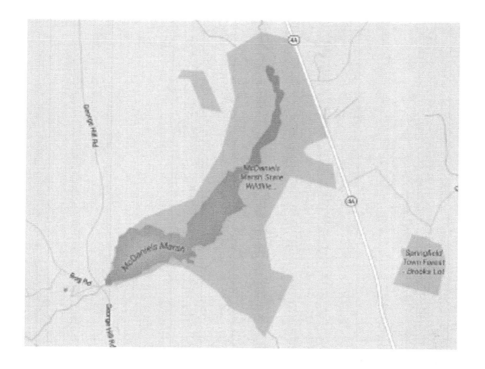

Figure 134 - Map of McDaniel's Marsh

We began our paddle close to the western shore. McDaniel's Marsh is generally shallow water with many floating islands of grass and muck. Its name "marsh" is very appropriate.

Two Bald Eagles

Within five minutes of our put-in Mike spotted a bald eagle. We sat quietly bobbing in the water, watching our symbol of American freedom on her/his tall treetop perch. Mike whispered again, "Look, another eagle."

We watched both birds and listened to the second bird call from its perch. Then the first eagle flew to the tree of the second eagle. The birds sort of danced along the same branch in a "let's get to know each other better" fashion.

Figure 135 - 3.5-yr old female bald eagle

Figure 136 - 1.5 - 2.5-yr old male bald eagle

My bald eagle email inquiry to the NH Audubon Society was responded to by Chris Martin, Raptor Biologist. *"The bird on the top is a 3.5-yr old (hatched Spring 2012) based upon its whitish head and dark mask and some dark spots on tips of tail feathers. It is probably a female based on its slightly chunkier size. The mottled brown bird on the bottom is a 1.5 - 2.5-yr old (hatched Spring 2013) based on its yellowing beak, whitish crown, and overall mottled appearance. Possibly a male as it appears to be slimmer. It's pretty unlikely that they are related to each other, in fact they are probably in transit, as most younger-aged eagles are during the Fall."*

Chris asked if I had any other pictures that might show if the eagles had leg identification bands. Upon receipt of my additional pictures, Chris emailed he could not see bands on either bird.

I shared with Chris the picture of the bald eagle I took last winter (Blog here) and he identified "the image clearly shows a silver band right leg and an orange band left leg, which signifies an eagle banded in Massachusetts, likely when it was a chick. Also shows a rather gutsy crow."

Figure 137 - Beaver Lodge in left of picture

Signs of beaver were everywhere – from floating beaver chews to lodges both close to shore and self-standing. The shorelines showed beaver paths into the woods where they were seeking trees and limbs for their winter food sources.

Figure 138 – Muskrat Pushup

Later we would see muskrat pushups – they somewhat resemble smaller beaver lodges neatly protruding two or three feet above the waterline.

We saw a greater or lesser yellowlegs, which are two rather similar-looking species.

Figure 139 – Yellowlegs

Statistics and References on McDaniel's Marsh Wild Management Area
http://www.wildlife.state.nh.us/maps/wma/mcdaniels-marsh.html

- **Approximately 2 miles in length and ¼ mile max width.**

- **Town:**Grafton, Springfield **County:** Grafton

- **Acres:**609

Bald Eagles

(http://www.wildlife.state.nh.us/wildlife/profiles/bald-eagle.html)

Bald eagles are legally protected in New Hampshire. Possession and take (which includes harming, harassing, injuring and killing) is illegal.

Distribution: Bald eagles are present year round in NH with pairs breeding and raising young in the spring/summer and many wintering in areas with open water such as Great Bay.

Description: 3' tall with a 6-8' wing span. Females weigh up to 14 lbs; males weigh 7-10 lbs. Immature bald eagles are mottled light brown, tan, and white until age 3 or 4. They have brown eyes, a black beak, and yellow feet. Adult bald eagles have a distinctive white head and white tail feathers, and a dark brown body and wings. Their eyes are pale yellow and the powerful beak and unfeathered feet are bright yellow.

Voice: Weak, high-pitched, chatters or whistles.

Habitat: Bald eagles breed in forested areas near bodies of water and winter near open water (i.e. coastal areas, rivers, and lakes with open water).

Nesting: Bald eagles can live up to 30 years of age and can begin breeding between 4-6 years of age. They build large nests in tall trees near the water's edge. Females lay 1-3 eggs in March - May. Both the male and female incubate the eggs, and the young hatch after five weeks. Bald eagles often retain the same mate for many years and reuse the same nest from year to year.

Diet: Primarily fish; occasionally other birds, small to medium mammals, turtles and even carrion.

Muskrat Pushups
(https://en.wikipedia.org/wiki/Muskrat)

Muskrat families build nests, called pushups, to protect themselves and their young from cold and predators. When we first spotted from a distance these muskrat pushups, we thought they were beaver lodges as they are somewhat similar, but not as large. In marshes, push-ups are constructed from vegetation and mud. These muskrat push-ups are up to 3 ft in height.

References

- **Kayaking McDaniel's Marsh Wildlife Management Area - Springfield, NH http://outdooradventurers.blogspot.com/2015/11/kayaking-mcdaniels-marsh-wildlife.html**

- http://www.wildlife.state.nh.us/maps/wma/mcdaniels-marsh.html

- http://www.wildlife.state.nh.us/wildlife/profiles/beaver.html

- http://www.wildlife.state.nh.us/wildlife/profiles/bald-eagle.html

- http://www.nhaudubon.org/about/centers/mclane/

- www.nhaudubon.org

- https://en.wikipedia.org/wiki/Muskrat

- **https://www.allaboutbirds.org/search/?q=Greater%20 Yellowlegs**

Welch-Dickey Loop Trail - A Training Hike for Mt Katahdin

In the fall, five friends and I would hike **Mt Katahdin** in Maine's **Baxter State Park**. Mt Katahdin is the northern terminus of the Appalachian Trail. One of the trails leading to the summit is known as **The Knife Edge**.

We expected this hike to be between nine (9) and eleven (11) hours over very rough terrain. We must be physically fit. As preparation for this trip, our group would do hikes of varying distances and difficulties. Each hike offers unique and beautiful scenery of New Hampshire. Our focus was on endurance and distance.

We carried day packs containing similar contents that we would carry on our Katahdin climb. We carried the same amount of water we would need for the Katahdin hike as well as other gear (e.g. at least 48 ounces of water, rain coat, winter hat, first aid pack, whistle, map, compass, camera, two light sources (flashlights and headlamps), duct tape, two 30 gal contractor for emergency shelter, bivy sack.)

We carry as a minimum what are known as the ten essentials for hiking http://www.outdoors.org/recreation/hiking/hiking-essentials.cfm.

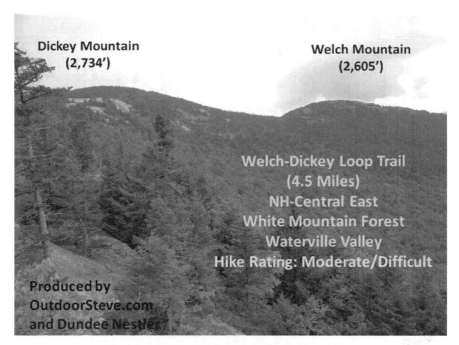

Figure 140 - Welch-Dickey Overview

For five weeks my hiking partners and I did a variety of training hikes:

- Mt Sunapee's Rim Trail to Lake Solitude – 3.5 hours

- Mt Sunapee's ski lift trail with a return on the Access Road. I did this route twice on two different days - 3.5 hours

- The 7.5 mile round trip Pumpelly Trail of Mount Monadnock - 8 hours

- South Mountain of Uncanoonuc - 2.5 miles in 2.5 hours

- 4.5 mile Welch-Dickey Loop Trail - 4 .5 hours

Let me share the Welch-Dickey Loop Trail.

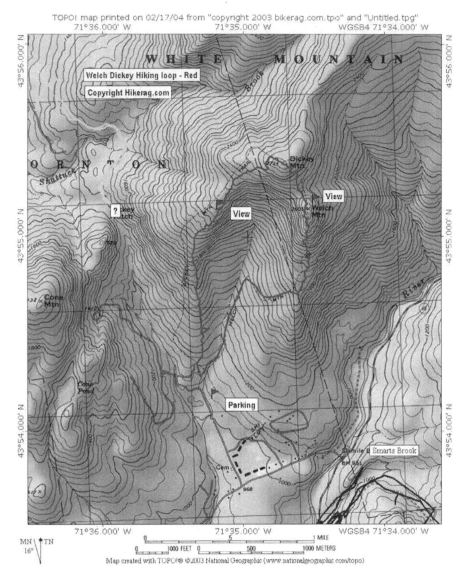

Figure 141 - Map of our Welch-Dickey Hike

I took the Welch-Dickey trail description from the **Hike New England** web site:
http://www.hikenewengland.com/WelchDickey030719.html

Mountains: Welch Mtn. (2605'), Dickey Mtn. (2734')
Trail: Welch-Dickey Loop Trail
Region: NH - Central East
White Mountain National Forest, Waterville Valley

Location: Thornton, NH
  Rating: Moderate/Difficult

Route Summary

This is a loop hike across the summits of Welch and Dickey Mountains, providing many views along the way as the trail winds its way across open ledges. It follows the yellow-blazed Welch-Dickey Loop Trail all the way. The different branches of the loop are commonly referred to as Welch Mountain Trail (the right-hand fork which leads most directly to Welch); and Dickey Mountain Trail (the left-hand fork which goes directly to Dickey Mountain.)

Figure 142 - Welch-Dickey Trail Sign

- Start on the Welch-Dickey Loop Trail, which will fork after just 15 yards.

- Take the right-hand branch to approach Welch Mountain first. (The return trip will be via the opposite leg.)

189

- After 1.3 miles on the Welch-Dickey Loop Trail, you will reach the open ledges and extensive views on the southern flank of Welch Mountain.

- Continue following Welch-Dickey Loop Trail and you will reach the summit of Welch Mountain 0.6 mile later where you will be treated to a 360-degree panorama.

- Descend the opposite side of the peak, continuing to follow the Welch-Dickey Loop Trail in a northerly direction.

- You will then need to do some uphill climbing before reaching the summit of Dickey Mountain 0.5 mile from Welch's peak. Dickey Mountain offers views of Franconia Ridge and Franconia Notch. Shortly before the summit, there will be a poorly marked 0.2-mile spur path on the right leading to an open ledge also with an outlook to the north.

- Still on Welch-Dickey Loop Trail, descend from Dickey's peak in the opposite direction from which you climbed it.

- After 2.1 miles, you are back at the fork near the beginning of the loop. Bear right to return to the parking lot.

Click the below 8 minute video as Dundee and I share our training for the Katahdin climb by hiking the Welch-Dickey Loop Trail.

References
Video and Blog: Welch-Dickey Loop Trail - A Training Hike for Mt Katahdin
http://outdooradventurers.blogspot.com/2013/08/in-september-2013-fourfriends-and-i.html.

Knife Edge Trail to Baxter Peak at Northern Terminus of Appalachian Trail

Six friends planned a long day of hiking, only to find a day and evening of climbing. The plan seemed relatively simple:

1. **Hike to Baxter Peak, the northern terminus of the 2,162 mile Appalachian Trail (AT)** [1].
2. **Cross the fabled 1.1 mile Knife Edge Trail.**
3. **Hike five miles on the AT starting at its northern terminus, Baxter Peak.**

Our ultimate achievement through endurance and teamwork brought more satisfaction because of the challenges and time on the mountain. Below are comments, maps, pictures, and videos and our climb. Our Mt. Katahdin accomplishment was both physically and mentally demanding. I am extremely proud of my fellow adventurers and how we worked together for this team triumph.

Mount Katahdin is the highest mountain in Maine at 5,269 feet. Named Katahdin by the Penobscot Indians, the term means "The Greatest Mountain". It is part of the Appalachian Mountain range and is located in Baxter State Park. Baxter State Park is a large wilderness area permanently preserved as a state park, located in Piscataquis County in north-central Maine. It covers 327 square miles.

The Knife Edge was the highpoint of our trip, but the descent from Pamola Peak was nearly as challenging as we had to use technical rock climbing skills.

---

[1] The precise length of the Appalachian Trail changes over time as sections are modified or rerouted.

Figure 143 - Baxter Peak – Northern Terminus of AT

Figure 144 - The Knife Edge Trail

Our trip started at Roaring Brook campground on the Chimney Pond Trail at 6:45 am. We arrived at Chimney Pond Campground after a 2 hr 45 minute hike. From the Campground we took Dudley Trail to Pamola Peak. We had to do a 40 foot straight down descent grabbing cracks in the granite rocks while seeking spots for footholds.

That was immediately followed by climbing straight up 40 feet to Chimney Peak. Admittedly, this 80 foot traverse was the most challenging section for this author. Once atop Chimney Peak we climbed and scooted the 1.1 mile Knife Edge Trail. This brought us to South Peak, then to the summit, Baxter Peak.

Our 15 hour trip was an unrelenting 11.5 miles. We finished the last two hours of the decent in darkness with only our headlamps illuminating the strewn boulder trail.

Enjoy the below videos of our Mount Katahdin hike.

Detail Videos of Knife Edge, Google Route, and Overview on Our Katahdin Trek

- Sit back, Click Here for our Knife Edge half hour video, and enjoy **- and cringe** - as we cross the fabled Knife Edge Trail.

- Bedford Community Television (BCTV) is now showing the Knife Edge to Baxter Peak at the Northern Terminus of the Appalachian Trail produced by OutdoorSteve.com

- Click here for a narrated Map of our Katahdin Trail Route using Google Earth.

- Click here for A Little Stroll Along Katahdin with Dundee and LoonsNest.biz

Figure 145 - Map - Roaring Brook to Katahdin Stream via Knife Edge Trail and Baxter Peak and AT

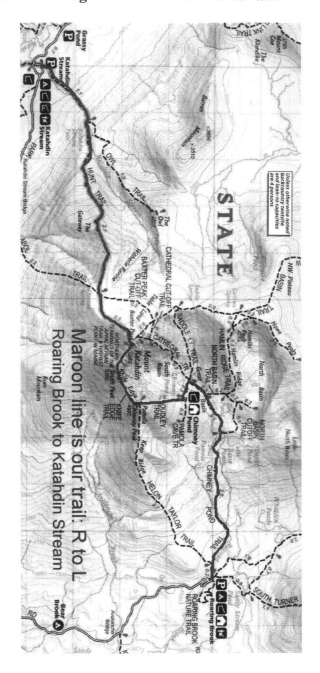

Figure 146 - Mt Kathadin Hike: Trail Miles and Times Table

Trails	Start	End	Hours and Miles	Comments
Roaring Brook Campground to Chimney Pond Campground	Start 6:45 am	9:30 am	2 ¾ hrs 3.3 miles	Chimney Pond Trail an easy hike. Four of us used trekking poles. Some nice side trail views.
Chimney Pond Campground to Pamola Peak via Dudley Trail	10 am	1 pm	3 hrs 1.4 miles	After a snack and rest at Chimney Pond Campground, we tied our trekking poles to our packs. The Dudley Trail is a 2,000 foot elevation gain and a relentless massive granite boulder laden trail nearly straight up. The Dudley Trail required our hands for pulling, grabbing rocks and hand holds, our legs for pushing, our arms for lifting our bodies, our feet for pushing and toe holds, and our butts to slide down granite formations. We were exhausted when we reached Pamola Peak. Indeed it was a very trying physical test of our mettle.
Pamola Peak to Chimney Peak/Knife Edge	1:20 pm	2:12 pm	¾ hrs	Our descent down the 40 foot drop from Pamola Peak was technical "rock climbing". We held indentations in the rocks while reaching for footholds. Indeed for this descent we used hands, arms, body and butt.
Knife Edge to South Peak	2:12	3:00 pm	3/4 hrs .8 miles	A .8 mile balancing act along the ridge of the Knife Edge Trail. Prior to this trip I had visions of panicking because of the elevation and the 2 to 3 thousand foot drop-offs and extremely narrow trail. Truthfully, I had no fear as I crossed the Knife Edge trail.

Continue to Trails Page 2 of 2

195

Page 2 of 2 Trails	Start	End	Hours and Miles	Comments
South Peak to Baxter Peak	3:00	3:50 pm	3/4 hrs .3 miles	This ridge trail went up and down. Just when we got to the top of the trail, it would drop and we would start another descent. Then an ascent followed by another descent. We were close to 7 hours since we left Roaring Brook campground and were tired. At each high ledge we could see Baxter Peak, but could not differentiate the cols in the undulating ridge.
From Baxter Peak via the Hunt Trail across the Katahdin Tablelands	4:00 pm	5:15 pm	1 ¼ hrs 1.0 miles	The Tablelands were like a country hike. It was flat and a welcome respite. We passed the famous Henry David Thoreau Spring. We had been hiking for nearly ten hours at this point.
Hunt Trail after the Tablelands to Katahdin Stream Campground	5:15 pm	10:00 pm	4 3/4 hrs 4.2 miles	We were now headed down and homeward bound, BUT still had 4.2 miles according to the trail sign. The first two miles were a steep descent over rough granite terrain. We did have some technical areas. One section had steel handles embedded in the granite pluton to make the descent from huge ledges a bit easier. It took us two hours just to get below the tree line. At 8:30 pm we put on our headlamps. We used our trekking poles to give us stability in navigating the descending rock strewn path. At 10 pm we reached the ranger check-in station where we "signed-out" in the register that the six of us were safely down off the mountain. We also met the Park Ranger who had been told by two people with headlamps whom had passed us earlier in the dark that we were fine and on our way.
TOTAL HOURS and TOTAL MILES	6:45 am	10:00 pm	15 hours 11.5 miles	What a Journey!!! Definitely a Bucket List accomplishment

Knife Edge Trail

The Knife Edge Trail is perhaps the most spectacular trail in New England – and also the most dangerous. It would take us two hours to cross from Chimney Peak to South Peak.

196

To get to the start of the Knife Edge Trail, we had hiked 6 ½ hours from our Roaring Brook campsite. Three of these hours were spent on rock strewn Chimney Pond Trail; then three hours on a very rugged and prolonged steep Dudley Trail to reach Pamola Peak. The last half hour was a very technical Pamola descent and then we ascended Chimney Peak. We were now at the start of the almost mile high 1.1 mile long Knife Edge Trail. Whew!

We were advised to avoid the Knife Edge in stormy weather. The exposure to high winds, rain, and lightning is extreme. We were warned that once we decided to cross the Knife Edge, we MUST STAY on that trail. There is no safe way to descend off either side of this mountain ridge. The drop is 2,000 feet off one side and 3,000 feet off the other.

The mile long path stretches across the South Basin's headwall between Pamola and Baxter Peak. I believe you will get a sense of what these six outdoor enthusiasts experienced crossing this unique narrow mile-high ridge with multi 1,000 foot drops on both sides. At one point for about 20 feet, the width of the ridge was close to 18 inches. The views, when we dared a birds-eye glimpse, were magnificent and certainly breathtaking.

References

- **Video and Blog:** Knife Edge Trail to Baxter Peak at Northern Terminus of Appalachian Trail
http://outdooradventurers.blogspot.com/2014/08/hiking-from-roaring-brook-campground-to_25.html

- www.baxterstateparkauthority.com/

- The Wilderness Map Company, Franconia, NH 03580 (I could find no web site on the map I used titled, **Katahdin: Baxter State Park, Maine**)

- OutdoorSteve Blog Post November 2009: Springer Mountain, Georgia - The Southern Terminus of the Appalachian Trail

- Appalachian Trail Conservancy

Figure 147 - Three Mt Katahdin Goals Accomplished

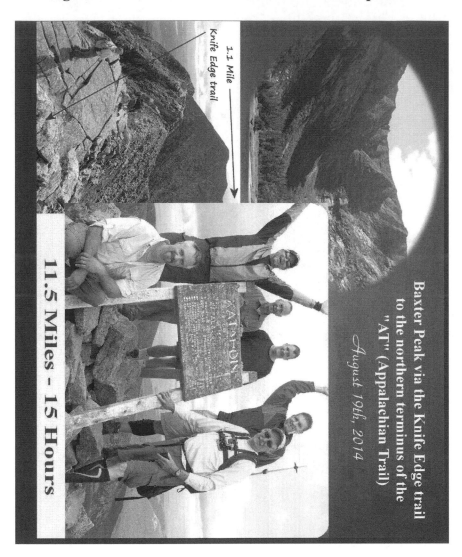

Hiking Mount Major for Panorama View of Lake Winnipesaukee

Figure 148 - Lake Winnipesaukee from Summit of Mount Major

Mount Major is 1,785 feet in elevation and located in central New Hampshire. It overlooks Alton bay on the southwest shore of Lake Winnipesaukee.

George and I took a loop trail beginning and ending at the parking lot off route 11. From the back, left-hand corner of the Route 11 parking lot, we took the orange blazed Boulder Loop Trail. Boulder Loop Trail is about 1.6 miles from the parking lot to the summit of Mount Major.

Boulder Loop Trail climbs easily at first then gets steeper over rocky ledges. Huge boulders block the trail and are passable only by squeezing your body through narrow slots in the rocks. After a final steep climb, we began to see some views of Lake Winipeasaukee. It took about another 15 minutes to reach the summit and the remains of a stone built hiker hut. Our total time form parking lot to summit was about 90 easy going minutes.

The granite laden summit overlooks beautiful Lake Winnipeasaukee. The view below to our right is Alton Bay with an across the lake view of the town of Wolfboro. We take in the breath-taking sights of some of the 258 islands on the lake, and its 182 mile shoreline. The lake is 72 square miles, and about 21 miles long and 9 miles at its widest point, so we really got a nice taste of the beauty of this gem of New Hampshire

Our descent from the summit was on the blue blazed Mt Major Trail. The Boulder loop orange-blazed trail junctions with the blue blazed Mt Major Trail at the summit (be aware the Beaver Pond Trail also meets at the summit so check your map.)

Our total trip was about 3 hours which includes a half hour on the summit. Certainly this is a family hike mountain for all ages.

Statistics
Elevation: 1,785' (544m)
Prominence: 187' (57m)
Mountain range: Belknap Mountains
Location: Central New Hampshire, USA
Area of water surface: 72 square miles
Number of islands: 258
Distance around lake: 182 miles
Height above sea level: 504 feet
Overlooks Lake Winnipesaukee

References
- **Video and Blog:** Hiking Mount Major for a Panorama View of Lake Winnipesaukee: http://tiny.cc/owp74x
- Hike New England http://tiny.cc/oaq74x
- Lake Winnipesaukee http://tiny.cc/djq74x

2011 Goffstown Giant Pumpkin Weigh-off & Regatta

Figure 149 - Giant Pumpkin Weigh-Off & Regatta

"Pull over, there's a giant pumpkin in the river with a person sitting in it!" my wife said as we were passing over the Piscataquog River in Goffstown, New Hampshire. She had spotted a weird scene. Lo and behold there were several giant pumpkins on the river - and they appeared to be racing each other! We were in the mist of the Goffstown Giant Pumpkin Weigh-off and Regatta.

Jim Beauchemin is a volunteer organizer of the Goffstown Giant Pumpkin Weigh-off and Regatta. I saw Jim's license plate and I asked him, "What does **1,314 LBS** mean?" He enthusiastically told me his giant pumpkin had won first prize at the 2005 Topsfield Fair and his plate number was the weight of his winning giant pumpkin.

Figure 150 - Winner of the Largest Giant Pumpkin - 1,465 lbs

Because of my prior year glimpse of this unique parade of giant pumpkins on the Piscataquog, and Jim's enthusiasm for this hobby/sport, I made it my quest to see this year's Goffstown Giant Pumpkin Weigh-off and Regatta "upfront and personal."

Here is my whirlwind tour of my two days at the Giant Pumpkin Weigh-off and Regatta:

The New Hampshire Giant Pumpkin Growers Association (NHGPGA) Hosts the Weigh-off

o Front-end loaders carry the giant pumpkins for the weigh-off from their pallets to the scale.

o Jim Beauchemin was the narrator and skillfully kept the crowd's enthusiasm throughout the weigh-off and educated them to giant pumpkin growing.

o Bruce Hooker of Belmont, NH was the winning grower. His

pumpkin weighed 1,465 lbs

The Goffstown Giant Pumpkin Regatta is a Boat Race on the Piscataquog River

o Because an excessive amount of rainfall in a short period of time this summer caused many giant pumpkins to grow too fast and split, there was a fear among the Regatta organizers that there would not be enough pumpkins to use as boats this year. Thankfully, several of the growers donated giant pumpkins for use in the Pumpkin Regatta.

At 2 pm the giant pumpkin boat building started

Figure 151 - Giant Pumpkins Carved for Electric Motor

o Bruce Normand expertly guided and supervised the process for "Giant Pumpkin" boat carving and river testing.

o The first boat building task is to use a plywood template and a power saw to cut a two foot or so diameter hole in the top of the pumpkin.

o Only the grower is allowed to remove the seeds from the giant pumpkins, as the seeds can be very valuable. I heard anywhere from $800 to $1,600 per seed from winning giants.

o Bolts attach the plywood around the carved opening and the wood serves as a platform to connect an electric motor.

o Each team has a boat theme. You will see their designs in my video.

Sunday morning each team is assigned a time to test their boats on the Piscataquog River

Figure 152 - Goffstown Fire and Rescue Readies Safety Boats

o The boats are ballasted with sand. Insufficiently ballasted boats tend to tip, or heel, and can result in capsizing.

o The electric motors and batteries were placed on/in the boat.

o The captains take the boats for a maiden voyage.

o This maiden voyage is as much fun to watch as the actual race itself. Some of the captains had never been in a giant pumpkin before, and you could feel the nervousness in the air.

o The support crews were tremendous with their encouragement and support for all contestants.

Figure 153 - A Captain Takes Her Boat for a Trial Run

o Goffstown Fire and Rescue handled water safety. The Goffstown hydro dam is very near to the start of the race. In case of capsizing, to catch the "captains" of each pumpkin from going over the dam, two safety catch lines were strung across the river just upstream from the dam.

o The Goffstown Chief of Fire and Rescue reviewed the safety issues with all captains.

At 3 pm the Cannon Roared and Nine Giant Pumpkins headed toward the Goffstown Main Street Bridge

o Upon the roar of the starting cannon, and with the dam at their backs, the captains aimed their giant pumpkin boats upstream into the strong current. Their target was the Main Street Bridge finish line.

Some of the boats swirled in circles, others seemed to be pushed downstream with the current, and one, specifically the Goffstown News Harry Potter themed boat, kept river left aiming straight at the bridge.

Figure 154 - A Boat Captain Fires T-Shirts to the Crowd

o The Giant Pumpkin Eater suddenly appeared upstream honking its horn with water hoses spraying the boats. Indeed some of the boats reciprocated with their own hoses. We had a Regatta "Battle on the Piscataquog" – all in fun.

o To fire up the river-bank spectators, some of the boats used air-cannons to shoot Goffstown Regatta monogrammed t-shirts into the crowd.

Figure 155 - Giant Pumpkin Eater Puts the Fleet Under Attack

o The winner of the 2011 Giant Pumpkin Regatta was the Harry Potter themed boat of the Goffstown News. Actually, all the boat captains are winners. Meeting the challenge of steering a near-thousand pound pumpkin, seated on their battery with knees up, and reaching back in an awkward position to steer and throttle – showed me that there should be nine trophies awaiting all finishers of the Giant Pumpkin Regatta.

An international flair was present throughout the two days as a TV crew from Germany did interviews and videos.

Figure 156 - And the Winner is Harry Potter!!

- Thanks to the support of the New Hampshire Giant Pumpkin Growers Association and countless sponsors and volunteers throughout Goffstown, the Giant Pumpkin Weigh-off and Regatta has become the signature event for Goffstown Main Street. I can't wait to attend next year.

I now will never have to say, "I wish I had watched the Goffstown Giant Pumpkin Weigh-off and Regatta".

References

o Jim Beauchemin's Discovery Channel DVD, "**The Secrets of Growing Champion Giant Pumpkins**", is available at https://www.createspace.com/209048. It is an entertaining presentation with a wealth of information on growing giant pumpkins.

o **Excess Rain, Lack of Growers** http://tiny.cc/djq74x
o **Goffstown Reviews the Seedy Fleet** http://tiny.cc/oev74x

o New Hampshire Giant Pumpkin Growers Association
http://www.nhgpga.org/

o Goffstown Main Street
http://www.goffstownmainstreet.org/

o World Record Giant Pumpkin is 2,009 lbs as of October 1, 2012 held by Ron Wallace of Greene, RI.

Video Reference Goffstown Giant Pumpkin Regatta
- **Blog: Giant Pumpkin Regatta**
  http://outdooradventurers.blogspot.com/2011/10/goffstown-nh-giant-pumpkin-weigh-off.html
- **Video Giant Pumpkin Weigh-off and Regatta**
  http://www.youtube.com/watch?feature=player_embedded&v=upw0o6B9JBo

October 2014 Goffstown, NH Giant Pumpkin Regatta

Figure 157 - We love our pumpkins!

This 20 minute video documents the wonderful celebration of Fall shared with the local communities by the town of Goffstown, New Hampshire. A giant pumpkin weigh-in Saturday morning (the winner was 1,284 lbs) was followed by an afternoon of carving and decorating a selection of these same giant pumpkins in preparation for the next day' s Sunday afternoon Giant Pumpkin Regatta.

A Giant Pumpkin Regatta is a unique experience to see as captains dressed in unique costumes paddle inside giant 1,000 lb pumpkins up the Piscataquog River in a race solely for bragging rights "For best giant pumpkin boat."

Figure 158 - Giant Pumpkin Weigh-off

Day 1

- Morning Giant Pumpkin Weigh-off (Winner 1,284 lbs)

- Afternoon Carving and Decorating of the Giant Pumpkins for the Sunday's Giant Regatta

- Apple Sling Shot Contest

- Learning to use a Fire Extinguisher

- Physical Exercise Contest

- Giant Pumpkin Boat Building

- Fireman Mini-muster

Figure 159 - The Giant Pumpkin Race Starting Line

Day 2

- Pie Eating Contest

- Small Pumpkin River Race

- Giant Pumpkin Regatta

References

- **Video and Blog: Goffstown, NH Giant Pumpkin Regatta**
  http://outdooradventurers.blogspot.com/2014/11/octobe
  r-18-19-2014-goffstown-nh-giant.html
- **Goffstown Giant Pumpkin Weigh-off**
  http://outdooradventurers.blogspot.com/2011/10/goffstown
  -nh-giant-pumpkin-weigh-off.html.
- More of Outdoor Steve's blog posts can be seem
  at http://www.outdoorsteve.com.

Lake Umbagog – a Gem in the Great North Woods

Figure 160 - Lake Umbagog - The Border Between NH and ME and the Headwaters of the Androscoggin River

Ominous dark clouds were overhead. White caps on Lake Umbagog were building. The wind was gusting. Do John, Dundee and I continue paddling north three miles, or do we head back to our campsite?

We had left our Big Island remote camp two hours earlier paddling on the west shore of Lake Umbagog with the plan to reach the northern end of the eight mile long lake, and then return south to our campsite via the east shore. On the way we would explore the headwaters of the Androscoggin River and the terminus of the Magalloway River.

Fortunately, we heeded a fellow paddler's storm warning, and decided to do a one-mile paddle across the lake to Tyler Point before heading south. Or did we delay our turnabout too long?

Planning the Trip

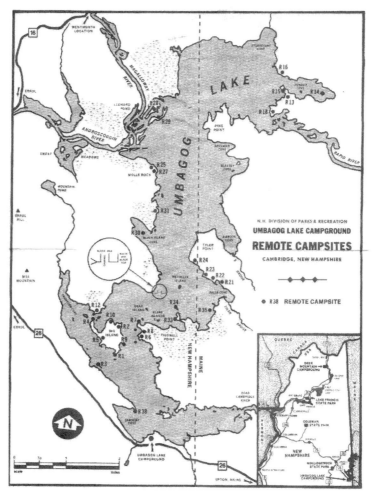

Figure 161 - Map: Lake Umbagog

Weather is always a major consideration for us. Originally we planned to do a ten-hour hike in Baxter State Park, Maine to the terminus of the northern end of the Appalachian Trail. Two days of heavy weather were forecast, and we decided against this trek.

Dundee suggested paddling Lake Umbagog. We went to www.weather.com/ and www.noaa.gov/ for satellite views, and our consensus was the weather would be light scattered showers in the Lake Umbagog area.

The weather in this region can change rapidly, and the literature notes the lake can become very challenging in moderate to high winds. Regardless, we decided it was a go!

Lake Umbagog

The Lake straddles the border between Maine and New Hampshire. Lake Umbagog is 7,850 acres with a north-south length close to eight miles. Using Google Earth (www.google.com/earth/index.html) we estimated at least 12 miles of paddling hugging the western shoreline to the northern terminus of the lake. Shoreline campsites are operated by the State of NH. The web site to make reservations is http://newhampshirestateparks.reserveamerica.com/

The Lake Umbagog State Park offers 34 remote campsites in isolated locations around the lake accessible only by boat. Wildlife viewing includes deer, moose, loons, eagles, osprey, and other varieties of birds.

For more information about canoeing and kayaking Lake Umbagog go to http://www.fws.gov/northeast/lakeumbagog/boating.html

To see a Lake Umbagog map with its 34 remote sites go to http://netrailhead.com/nh/sp/umbagog.html

The Trip - Day 1

We arrived at Lake Umbagog State Park in early afternoon for three days of paddling and camping. Two park rangers welcomed us and were most accommodating. Upon our comment to them that we wanted to paddle the whole lake and were seeking a remote site to help us accomplish our goal, they suggested campsite 4 on the north side of Big Island. Big Island is about three miles up the lake from our put-in at the southern tip of the lake.

Our paddling crafts: John (Old Town Cayuga 110 kayak), Dundee (Grumman 15' aluminum canoe) and I (Old Town Adventure 139 kayak).

We paddled north near the western shore, and arrived at our campsite in about two hours. We set up our tents, including tarps over the camp table to protect us from rain. We started a fire in the fire ring, and relaxed to enjoy our earthly presence on this remote wilderness island.

Day 2

We awoke at 6 am. Chief Chef John made a delicious egg, bacon and cheese omelet wrapped in tortilla shells. These, along with Dundee's coffee, made a great start for the day. By 9 am we were paddling north along the western shore. The wind was calm and the water was smooth as glass.

Around 11 am we reached Black Island cove. The wind had begun to pick up and the lake became choppy with small waves forming. Fortunately, we heeded a camper's advice to abandon our trip north and to head back to camp as the wind was expected to increase and the already rough waters to build even higher. We still wanted to see as much of the southern half of the lake as we could, and we felt we could return safely on the eastern side of the lake. We paddled across the lake to Tyler Point with the easterly wind and with the waves at our backs. As Dundee said, "With the wind at our backs we were surfing fast across the tips of the wave crests. Yes, it was fantastic!"

We went ashore at Tyler Point, and there we introduced ourselves to Leonard and Camille, two brothers raised in the area. Leonard suggested on our return paddle we stop at Tyler Cove for a ¼ mile hike to a natural flowing spring.

Figure 162 - A Friendly Fellow Paddler Suggests we Stop at Tyler Cove on Our Return Paddle

Figure 163 - Sipping from the Fountain of Youth at Tyler Cove

The short hike to the spring at Tyler Cove was certainly worth our time, and as I scooped the delicious cold spring water into my mouth, I wondered if we had discovered the fountain of youth!

The wind was now gusting and causing us serious concerns, and the waves were rolling and splashing such that I had visions of an ocean launching of our kayaks and canoes at high tide. We now needed to prove our mettle to get back to our Big Island campsite. The wind was blowing directly at us, and we needed to go perpendicular to it in order to move south along the eastern shoreline. We used whatever protection from the shore and trees we could find to minimize our exposure to the strong winds and heavy rain now blowing across the lake from the west.

Dundee had the toughest paddle, as his aluminum canoe was like a sail in the wind. He had to paddle with his bow into the wind, at a near 90 degree angle in order to go parallel with the shoreline and not get swamped by the pounding waves. His paddling expertise and confidence were apparent as he gently moved along the shoreline.

John and I pointed our kayaks at a 45 degree angle into the western wind in order to move south. We both wore kayak skirts, but some water did manage to leak into our kayaks. Our hope was to not take on too much water in order to avoid the need to go ashore to bail the kayaks, or in the worst case scenario, end up being swamped. Bailing was nearly impossible in these winds and lake conditions. Constant paddling was needed to maintain both our direction and uprightness.

Indeed, after a three hour return paddle, we made it safely back to Big Island – a bit wet, but none-the-less without a "tip over". We had beaten the winds and white caps of Lake Umbagog.

Figure 164 - Our Big Island Campsite

We were drenched from the rain and water, and certainly cold, so once reaching our camp we immediately built a roaring campfire, changed into warm clothes, and boiled water for hot soup.

Never say, "I wish I had paddled Lake Umbagog".

We would certainly return to Lake Umbagog for another paddle to explore the northern half of the Lake, including the headwaters of the Androscoggin River to the Errol Dam, and the terminus of Lake Magalloway from the Lake Umbagog Wildlife Refuge on Route 16.

Certainly, we never have to say, *"I wish I had paddled Lake Umbagog."*

Figure 165 - Paddling Lake Umbagog

Video Reference Lake Umbagog Paddle and Tenting
• **Blog: Exploring Umbagog – a Gem in the Great North Woods**   http://outdooradventurers.blogspot.com/2010/ 09/exploring-lake-umbagog-gem-in-great.html

Touching a Paddle in Boundary Waters of Minnesota

Cathy said, "I want to visit Minnesota". So off we went.

We flew to Minneapolis, rented a car, and spent seven days traveling in northeastern Minnesota. We saw beautiful country, visited unique places in the Lake Superior area, and most of all we met wonderful Minnesotans. We now have new friends and great memories of Minnesota and the Boundary Waters Canoe Area Wilderness (BWCAW).

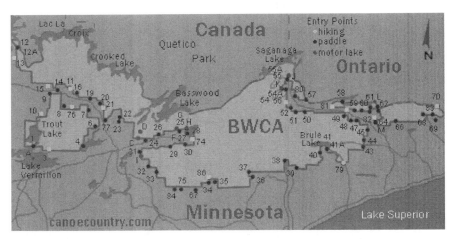

Figure 166 - Map of BWCAW: Minnesota and Ontario

The BWCAW is a region of wilderness straddling the Canada–United States border between Ontario and Minnesota. It is composed of over 1 million acres of forests and thousands of miles of water routes. No motorized vehicles or boats are allowed within the perimeters of this wilderness area. Permits are required for all visitors to the BWCA. A limited number of permits grant access to each BWCAW entry point.

Cathy and I spent three days in Ely, Minnesota at the Blue Heron Bed and Breakfast, close to entrance 31 of the BWCAW. Being in Ely provided us opportunities for:

- A two hour kayak paddle to South Farm Lake in BWCAW.

- A three hour canoe paddle from North Farm Lake into the Kawishiwi River, another entrance into the BWCAW.

- Visiting the **International Wolf Center** to see wolves in a two acre habitat. Attend a Wolf Howling seminar.

- Visiting the **North American Bear Center** and seeing black bears in their natural environment

- An evening at a lakeside campfire learning how to "howl" like a wolf to see if we could get a reciprocal howl from wild wolves that may be nearby.

Enjoy our **Video References** below as Cathy and I share a taste of the boundary waters and the Ely attractions. Two of our Minnesota friends will give you an upfront demonstration of wolf howling.

The following September friends and I will never have to say, "We wish we had paddled a week in the Boundary Waters Canoe Area."

To get more information on the boundary waters visit:

- **BoundaryWatersCanoeArea.com**
  http://www.BoundaryWatersCanoeArea.com

- **Discover Ely, MN**
  http://www.wolf.org/wolves/visit/visitingely.asp

- **CanoeKayak.com**
  http://www.canoekayak.com

International Wolf Center
http://www.wolf.org/wolves/

North American Bear Center
http://www.bear.org/website/

Video References: Researching Trip to Minnesota's Boundary Waters
- **Blog: Touching a Paddle in the Boundary Waters**
  http://outdooradventurers.blogspot.com/2010/10/touching-paddle-in-boundary-waters-of.html
- **Wolf Howling, Ely, Black Bears and Boundary Water Research**
  http://www.youtube.com/watch?feature=player_embedded&v=PsWzoIYVwvA

Paddling the Waters of Quetico Provincial Park

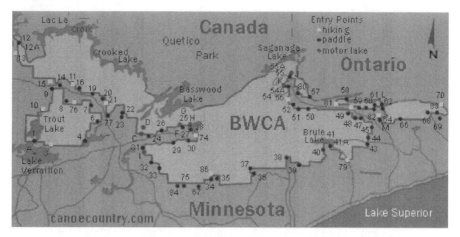

Figure 167 - Map: BWCA – Minnesota and Ontario

Quetico Provincial Park is a region of isolated Canadian wilderness straddling the Canada - United States border between southwestern Ontario and northern Minnesota. Quetico is composed of over 1 million acres of forests and thousands of miles of water routes. Permits are required for all visitors.

In mid-September, three outdoor enthusiast friends and I paddled a six day 35 mile loop in the Quetico Provincial Park region of Ontario.

We all agreed we had the most physically and technically demanding portages we have ever attempted. We balanced these challenges against seeing some of the most beautiful wilderness, pristine water, and wildlife in the country. Indeed, the boundary waters provided us with a very memorable and impressive paddling experience.

The Portages

Figure 168 - Canoe Shoulder Yoke for One Person Carry

We had seventeen portages for eight plus portage miles. (See the **Video References** below to see my spreadsheet for the lake sequences, their portages, and the portage distances).

My son Tim and I were in an 18' 6" 43 lbs kevlar ultra-light Wenona canoe, and Dundee and his son Paul in a similar model canoe. The portages were through dense woods with extremely narrow and rough granite rocks of all sizes and shapes, up and down hills, over fallen trees, mud, and water.

At each portage one person from each canoe carried the canoe on their shoulders using a leather padded neck yoke. I portaged the canoe 5 times, whereas Tim did the other 12 portages. Dundee and Paul likewise worked a similar type of division of labor to carry the canoe at each portage. Our backpacks (in each canoe - a food pack and two packs for each of our personal gear) averaged 50 plus lbs for the first few days until the food weight eased.

Figure 169 - Beginning a Gear Portage

To get the full feel of our physical effort of the seventeen portages, you must realize the four of us had to make three trips each across the portage. Because of the narrow and rough terrain and its length, each canoe was carried by one person, while their canoe partner carried the food pack. We then returned over the portage for the remaining gear to carry our personal packs and other hand carried gear such as paddles, fishing poles, tent, dry bag, and maps.

We had no injuries of hernia, sprained ankles or whatever. Amen!

As you see from the portage spreadsheet, our first day of paddling had the three longest portages, and since it was our first day, we had the heaviest weight of our entire trip. I must confess - after we selected a campsite on the Meadows Lake island, set up our tents, and went for a much needed refreshing swim - we all took a one hour nap. Exhaustion was upon us. Thereafter we began preparations for dinner.

Our Team

Figure 170 - Dundee and Paul Paddling Lake Agnes

Paul, our Meal Planner and Chief Cook, did a fabulous job in providing wonderful meals. My son Tim shared with Paul the meal preparation, camp setups, cleanup, etc.
Dundee was the navigator with excellent map reading skills and keeping us on our water trail as we paddled through fifteen or so lakes. There were no trail signs or lake signs – our only guidance was the detail map and our compass showing the portages– and Dundee's innate sense of direction and recognition of where we were in reference to the map.

As the days passed, we realized we were following a waterway highway as we portaged from lake to lake in a very logical manner.

Figure 171 - Just in Time to Get Out of the Rain and Snow

On all five of our evenings we slept on islands - as we felt this would provide more security from bear and wolves.

Wildlife and Indian Pictographs
We saw a variety of wildlife, including eagles, loons, mink, beaver, otter, grouse, signs of moose, heard wolf calls, and had warnings of black bear from Quetico rangers, but no sightings.

We saw ancient Ojibwe Indian pictographs (paintings on the lakeside granite) and petroglyphs (images etched into the granite) along the lakeside cliffs. We had bought a book, **Magic on the Rocks** by Michael Furtman on the Pictographs of Quetico, and we read the book in camp to educate ourselves on these little understood Ojibwe artifacts (http://tiny.cc/3ww74x).

Figure 172 - Paul Points to Ojibwe Pictographs

Figure 173 - Can You See the Four Pictographs Paul Sees?

Louisa Falls

We swam the first two days – day one off our island campsite in Meadows Lake and the second day in the middle of Louisa Falls - a one-hundred foot waterfall flowing from Louisa Lake into Agnes Lake. Halfway down the falls is a neat natural bathtub including a stream of water for a great back massage from the rushing water into the tub.

The following day we had a brief flurry of snow and cold rain, and of course, swimming was over. We fished as we paddled, but caught nothing of a size we could eat.

Forest Fire

There was a massive forest fire in the area - we could see and smell distant smoke from our island campsite on Summer Lake, but we were not in any danger. The Quetico ranger at Prairie Portage told us they generally leave these lightening started fires to burn out by themselves, as they are a natural process of the wilderness ecosystem.

Rough Water and Cold Weather

Figure 174 - From swimming to freezing within 24 hours

From Swimming Weather to Freezing Weather – Be Prepared!
We had three days of on and off heavy rain showers (including one shower of hailstones and snow) and 30 mph wind gusts and high waves as we crossed a few of the lakes. You ask, "Why did you cross in such rough conditions?" Well, we needed to seek a camp site for the night. These paddles absolutely required seasoned and strong paddlers, and thankfully we were all up to the task. There were no flips. Amen.

The Water
The Boundary Waters and Quetico lakes are pure, clear and pristine waters. Given the fact that the lakes were gouged out by the movement of mile thick glaciers thousands of years ago, the water depth frequently dropped off close to shore as the lakes were carved within granite mountains.

A question we frequently asked before the trip was "where do we get our drinking water while in the Quetico waters? Certainly boiling or purification tablets are the wisest recommendation for drinking any lake water. However, as we spoke to those who regularly paddle these waters, the feedback was "as you paddle in deep water, push your empty water containers as far down into the water as you can reach and then open the cap. Replace the cap before you bring the filled bottle back up. This water was of course boiled during cooking and using for hot beverages, but we drank directly from the bottles in which we stored the water.

Start a Campfire with Flint, Steel, Tinder – and Practice
One evening we played "survivor man" and started our campfire solely by use of flint and steel. A shower of sparks is needed to start a fire along with proper tinder (http://survivalcache.com/fire-tinder/) and - practice, practice and practice. I had brought a **FireSteel Scout** tool (www.lightmyfire.com) composed simply of flint and steel.

It's about as basic a process as you can ask for... people have been lighting fires with flint and steel for many, many years. But, again, it does require practice and the use of both hands.

I did start the fire with this tool, but I won't be throwing away my lighter and hand washing alcohol until I practice some more. The **FireSteel** makes a handy item in my pack for emergency situations. It does work in wet weather, but, it does take a knack.

Paul was the matchless fire starting expert in the group. Below, Paul demonstrates to how to start a fire with flint and steel. As Paul pointed out to us, the key is proper tinder i.e. (dried leaves, wood shaving chips, or, preferred if available, birds nests birch bark, and dry mosses) – and practice, practice and more practice.

Figure 175 - Flint, Steel and Tinder – and Practice

Trip Preparation
We entered the Canadian waters at the Prairie Portage location into Quetico Provincial Park via a water taxi tow on Moose Lake from Ely, MN. To assure the entry date we wanted, we needed to apply for an entry permit five months before our preferred date. There is a limited number of entry permits for each day. Piragis Northwoods Company in Ely coordinated our permit application,

outfitted us with two We-no-nah canoes, maps, food backpacks, and a large Duluth type backpack that could handle what I had originally packed into three dry bags. No motorized vehicles or power boats are allowed within the Quetico wilderness area.

Our Paddling Route

Figure 176 - Piragis Outfitters Shuttle us to Prairie Portage

Our six day water route was a loop of fifteen lakes within Quetico. From the Prairie Portage Ranger Station entry, we paddled north to Sunday Lake, then east to Meadows Lake, and then north on Agnes Lake until we reached the portage to Silence Lake. We looped back to Prairie Portage via the lake route known as the "S" chain of lakes: Silence, Sultry, Summer, Noon, Shade, West, South, and then to Basswood, Burke and Bayley Bay.

Although we passed through the northern Minnesota Boundary Waters Canoe Area Wilderness (BWCAW) as our canoes were towed with the motorboat, technically we did a Quetico paddling trip.

A Trip for the Physically Fit with a Planned Route

Our experience in the waters of Quetico taught us:

(1) You need to plan your portage route in agreement with the physical condition and paddling experience of your group. Develop your route considering portage length and portage frequency;

(2) This trip is for the physically fit outdoor enthusiast;

(3) You need strength and endurance paddling skills to handle long mileages and paddling amongst heavy wind and rough waves;

(4) A strong back for heavy, lengthy, and rough portages;

(5) Have at least one member of your group with map and compass reading skills. Remember Quetico has no trail signs or markers;

(6) Outdoor menu planning and cooking skills (at least one person);

Figure 177 - Our Take-out at Prairie Portage

(7) An ability to set up a campsite, start a campfire in different weather conditions (at least one person);

(8) A team mentality to work together in grinding and varying terrain and weather conditions and with camp setups;

(9) In our late September trip we went swimming one day – and the next day had to take shelter because of a snow and rain storm. Bring clothing appropriate for the time of year and any unpredictable changes in weather extremes;

(10) A sense of humor and enjoyment of the wonderful outdoors.

Figure 178 - A Big "Thank You" to Drew, Piragis Northwoods Outfitting Manager, for his outstanding advice and gear.

We all gained an appreciation for the beauty, tranquility and isolation of the Quetico area. Will we return? Yes - absolutely!

Now, I never have to say, "I wish I had paddled the boundary waters of Minnesota and Canada."

References

- Piragis Northwoods Outfitters http://www.piragis.com/

- Canoe On Inn http://www.canoeoninn.com/

- Bearwise http://www.mnr.gov.on.ca/en/Business/Bearwise/

- Boundary Water Canoe Access http://www.bwca.com/

- Boundary Waters Canoe Area & Quetico Provincial Park Canoe Trip Routes http://www.canadianwaters.com/boundary-waters-canoe-area-quetico-provincial-park-canoe-trip-routes/

- Mckenzie Maps http://www.bwcamaps.com/

- Quetico Provisional Park http://en.wikipedia.org/wiki/Quetico_Provincial_Park.

Video References Paddling Boundary Waters of Minnesota and Ontario
- **Blog:** Paddling the Waters of Quetico Provincial Park in Ontario **http://tiny.cc/4px74x**

- Video of Boundary Waters Portages http://tiny.cc/jtx74x
- Spreadsheet of lake sequences, portages and portage distances http://tiny.cc/e0x74x

Peak Foliage Paddling and Camping in the Green River Reservoir of Northern Vermont

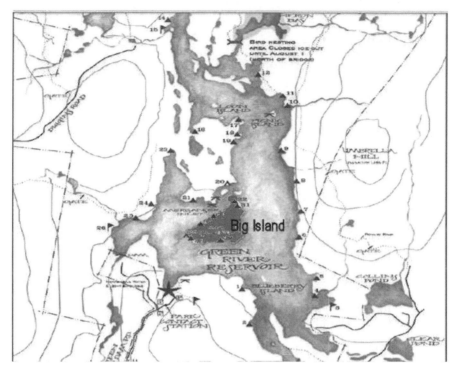

Figure 179 - Map of Green River Reservoir

Enjoy the below video and pictures of the magnificent foliage colors of northern Vermont.

In late September, five outdoor enthusiasts and I, using five kayaks and one canoe, did three days of paddling and two nights of tenting in the Green River Reservoir of northern Vermont.

Green River Reservoir became a state park in March 1999 when 5110 acres were purchased from the Morrisville Water and Light Department. This is not your typical Vermont State Park – Green River Reservoir provides camping and paddling experiences in a remote setting. All campsites can only be reached by paddling to them - some a 1 to 2-mile paddle from the launch site.

Figure 180 - Our Big Island Campsite

Figure 181 - Reflection on Water. Is Picture Upside Down?

The park will remain in its wild and undeveloped state, with low-impact, compatible recreational use allowed on and around the Reservoir. Management activities will be only those necessary to maintain the property's character, protect the environment and critical resources, demonstrate sustainable forest and wildlife management, control excessive recreational use, and ensure high-quality outdoor experiences for visitors.

Figure 182 - A Gorgeous Fall Day in Vermont

The 653-acre Reservoir includes about 19 miles of shoreline, one of the longest stretches of undeveloped shorelines in Vermont. Access to the park is in the southern part of the Reservoir off the Green River Dam Road. The Reservoir is designated as a "quiet" lake under Vermont "Use of Public Waters Rules." Boats powered by electric motors up to 5 mph and human-powered watercraft (canoes, kayaks, etc.) are the only ones allowed.

There are 28 remote campsites at various locations around the Reservoir. Camping is allowed only at designated campsites and can **only** be reached by boat. Each remote site has a maximum site occupancy based on the characteristics of the site. There is one designated group campsite that can accommodate up to 12 people.

Some campsites are closed each season and rehabilitated due to overuse through the years.

Figure 183 - See the Loon Eating a Fish

Figure 184- A Fabulous 3 Days in the Wilderness of Vermont

Video Resources Northern Vermont Fall Foliage
- Blog: Green River Reservoir
  http://outdooradventurers.blogspot.com/2012/10
  /peak-foliage-colors-paddling-and.html
- Lasting Memories of Colors in Northern
  Vermont
  http://www.youtube.com/watch?feature=player
  _embedded&v=wC8cLJ49nNQ
- Happy Birthday Linwood from Your Amigos
  http://youtu.be/aajYSMhpbgg

Springer Mountain, Georgia - Southern Terminus of the Appalachian Trail

Along with my sons Shaun and Tim, I visited Springer Mountain, Georgia, the southern end of the Appalachian Trail (AT). The Appalachian Trail Conservatory estimates the AT to be 2,175 miles, but yearly this figure changes with land ownership changes and limitations, and trail section relocations to mitigate foot path erosion. I have no urge to hike all of the AT (at least at this time), but given I was spending a month in Georgia, and I have hiked a great deal of the trail in New Hampshire, Maine, and Vermont, I could not resist hiking the Georgia terminus of the AT to see the two rock-embedded plaques.

Figure 185 - Southern AT Terminus Plaques

Some folks believe the AT was an Indian trail. That assumption is not true. In 1922 Benton MacKaye, a forester from Massachusetts had the vision of a continuous hiking trail from Georgia to Maine. . This wilderness footpath was recognized in 1937 and is maintained by thirty-two non-profit organizations.

Only about ten percent of all hikers - those who start from one end of the trail or the other - complete the entire trail in any given year. A thru-hiker can start at either of the trail's ends - Mount Katahdin, Maine or Springer Mountain, Georgia, but must complete the entire 2,175 +/- miles in one season or he/she is not a "thru-hiker", but will now become a "section-hiker".

The final (or beginning) mile of the AT passes through Forest Service Road (FSR) 42 near the top of Springer Mountain. From the small parking lot, you cross the FSR dirt road, locate the AT trail sign (with .9 miles engraved) and follow the vertical white painted rectangular (2 x 6 inch) trail markers to the AT's termination/beginning atop Springer Mountain. Visitors to the top of Springer Mountain can sign a logbook stored in a metal box encased in a rock holding one of the plaques.

Metal Box Springer Mt
Holding Terminus Log Book

Figure 186 - Southern Terminus Log Book

Benton MacKaye Trail

As we returned to the parking lot, we encountered the Benton MacKaye Trail. This is a four and ½-mile spur off the AT that essentially brings you back to the Springer Mountain parking lot. In tribute to Benton MacKaye, we decided to take this trail to return to the parking lot.

Figure 187 - The Southern Terminus Plague of the AT

Figure 188 - Benton MacKaye Trail Sign

Directions

It took many MapQuest searches, a few Google Earth reviews, and many Google Maps, before I found specific enough directions to Springer Mountain, the southern end of the AT. The Springer Mountain parking lot is located in the Chattahoochee National Forest nine-tenths (.9) miles from the top of Springer Mountain, where two rock-embedded plaques denote the southern end of the AT (note: There are many ways to get to the parking lot.)

Ten point four miles of a Wildness Road
Our last ten plus miles to the Springer Mountain parking lot were on a one-lane, rock-infested, mud holes galore, red dirt mountain road. Our bumpy ten mile per hour pace was jarring. We frequently had to pull off the road for on-coming cars. The road was literally cut into the side of the mountain with tall Georgia pines on each side. You surely need a four-wheel drive or SUV to use this route.

Figure 189 - Which Way to Springer Mountain?
Another approach path to the Appalachian Trail AT start/terminus on Springer Mountain is an arduous 8+ miles hike from Amicalola Falls State Park in North Georgia. See Springer Mountain Day Hike - Back Door to AT Southern Terminus for options to the summit of Spring Mountain (http://tiny.cc/cg574x)

Resources for AT Planning and Through-Hiker Experiences

A great resource to learn about the history of the AT, state by state trail maps, and how to plan the hike, can be located at www.appalachiantrail.org/. It takes the average AT thru-hiker six months to finish the entire trail.

Figure 190 - Valley from Southern Terminus of AT

Never Say, "I wish ..."

Shaun, Tim and I now, never have to say, "We wish we had been to the southern terminus of the AT."

References
- **Video and Blog:** Springer Mountain, Georgia - The Southern Terminus of the Appalachian Trail http://tiny.cc/2i574x
- Springer Mountain Day Hike - Back Door to AT Southern Terminus http://tiny.cc/cg574x

Do Mountain Lions Live in New Hampshire?

Figure 191 - Spot the Mountain Lion, Canada Lynx & Eagle

Squam Lakes Natural Science Center (http://www.nhnature.org/) in Holderness, NH is the place to go to see New Hampshire's wild animals "up close and personal".

The Sunday Union Leader announced a lecture at Squam Lakes on New Hampshire's large wildcats. Certainly, a topic of interest to all outdoor enthusiasts.

My wife Cathy and I arrived two hours before the 1 pm lecture so we could hike the ¾ mile Gephart Exhibit Trail. The Trail features live native New Hampshire wildlife in natural settings.

Yes, I had seen many of the animals and birds previously in their native habitat, but it was always for a fleeting moment. Now, Cathy and I are in awe seeing the same wildlife in their natural settings, and in an area where we can take pictures at our leisure, and read all about their traits.

Figure 192 - The Center is now their home

All the animals are in captivity, but in an environment close to their natural habitat and space needs. The above Red Fox, Black Bear, Barred Owl & Turkey Vulture were orphaned or injured before they came to the Center. The Center is now their home.

Never say, "I wish I wish I had seen and learned more about wildlife of New Hampshire."

So, are there mountain lions in NH? Hmm, maybe yes – maybe no. Plan a day at the **Squam Lakes Natural Science Center**

Video References
- Blog: Are Their Mountain Lions in New Hampshire?
  http://tiny.cc/tzm25x
- Squam Lakes Natural Science Center
  http://www.nhnature.org/

The Rocky Steps

Philadelphia Museum of Art - The 72 Steps of Victory

The 72 stone steps leading to the entrance of the Philadelphia Museum of Art in Philadelphia have become known as the "Rocky Steps". The steps were part of the triple-Oscar-winning film Rocky and four of its sequels, Rocky II, III, Rocky Balboa, and Rocky V. The eponymous character, Rocky, runs up the steps to the song "Gonna Fly Now".

Figure 193 - The Rock Statue- Philadelphia Museum of Art

References
- **Video and Blog:** The Rocky Steps
  http://outdooradventurers.blogspot.com/2013/12/the-rocky-steps.html
- The Rocky Steps
  http://en.wikipedia.org/wiki/Rocky_Steps

Making Apple Cider in New Hampshire with Robert Frost's, "After Apple Picking"

On a recent fall Sunday in Elkins, NH, family and friends had the pleasure of making apple cider while enjoying apple donuts, caramel covered apples, apple bobbing, and apple slices with cheese - all topped off with a reading of Robert Frost's poem, "**After Apple Picking**".

We made Apple Cider the New Hampshire way:
      1) Pick the apples
      2) Wash the apples
      3) Cut apples into four quarters
      4) Put quartered apples through a masher
      5) Press the mash for the apple cider.
      6) Bottle the cider
      7) Sip and enjoy the cider

Figure 194 - Living Robert Frost's "After Apple Picking"

Below is a video of our family oriented day making apple cider.

"Everyone must believe in something. I believe I'll go outdoors." – S. Priest

References
- **Video and Blog:** Making Apple Cider in New Hampshire with Robert Frost's, "After Apple Picking" http://outdooradventurers.blogspot.com/2013/10/making-apple-cider-in-new-hampshire.html

- **Bedford Community TV** Bedford Community TV (BCTV) is now playing **Making Apple Cider in New Hampshire with Robert Frost's, "After Apple Picking".** Check their Channel 16 schedule**.**

- Lea Newman, "**Robert Frost: The People, Places and Stories Behind His New England Poetry**" Amazon.com at http://tiny.cc/927m4w

- OutdoorSteve.com http://www.outdoorsteve.com

- Download a streaming video from *Bedford Community TV* channel 16 of **Making Apple Cider in New Hampshire with Robert Frost's, *"After Apple Picking"*** http://tiny.cc/m3384x

Kayaking the Herring River Estuary and Popponesset Bay of Cape Cod

Figure 195 - Herring River Estuary

Day 1: Kayaking the Herring River Estuary of Wellfleet and Truro

John invited Dundee and I to Cape Cod for two days of kayaking. Day one was planned to be a full day paddling around Wellfleet Harbor. However, our plan was short-lived when we explored the Herring River Estuary, a tidal river with a history of bygone prominence.

We proceeded west along the shoreline from the kayak landing next to the Wellfleet pier. As we neared Chequessett Neck Road and the dike at the mouth of the Herring River, John recalled a recent newspaper article on this dike. When it was built in 1909, it significantly reduced tidal flow to the salt marsh on the other side of the Road. This dike transformed the estuary into one of the Cape's most degraded natural resources.

Figure 196 - Map of our paddling route

Development of a restoration plan for the Herring River

In 2007 the Towns of Wellfleet and Truro and the Cape Cod National Seashore signed a Memorandum of Understanding to cooperate on the development of a restoration plan for the Herring River.

In a November 2015 article by Mary Ann Bragg of the Cod Times: "As it stands now the dike under the road has three 6-foot-wide culverts that are open during the outgoing tide. Only one of them - at 2 feet high - is open for the incoming tide. Generally, kayakers and canoeists carry their vessels up and over the road to continue their trips up or downstream.

Currently, the tidal range in the area of the dike is about 2½ feet, but if the salt marsh restoration project is fully implemented the tidal range could ultimately reach about 6½ feet. The tidal range is the vertical difference between the high tide and the succeeding low tide.

If the salt marsh restoration project is fully implemented as planned, all tide gates in the new dike would be removed and floating vessels would be able to pass freely up and down.

The Cape Cod National Seashore expects to release a final environmental impact statement winter of 2016 for the salt marsh restoration project. The fully restored backwaters of the river would cover about 890 acres, according to the latest estimates.

The restoration is meant to reverse some of the negative environmental outcomes of a decision in 1909 to build the first dike at Chequessett Neck Road. Some of the issues are bad water quality and fish kills, according to the draft environmental impact statement.

According to Cape Cod National ecologist Tim Smith, "Construction of the new dike with nine tidal gates, measuring 165 feet wide and 10 feet high, could begin in 2018 if all goes as planned. Planners want to steer paddlers away from trying to pass through the gates until the implementation is complete. That could take anywhere from two years to 20."

It is expected that when the existing tidal gate structure at the mouth of the Herring is replaced, along with other upstream considerations, this significant change will restore and provide full tidal flow to the Herring River Estuary and a promise for shell-fishing and other community opportunities." (http://tiny.cc/iuqn6x)

If you are interested in more information, or to stay up-to-date on the Herring River Estuary, please visit Friends of Herring River.. They have an email newsletter at http://tiny.cc/uz484x.

Paddling the Herring River Estuary
We decided it would be worth our effort to portage over Chequessett Neck Road and paddle up the Herring River. We had before us an opportunity to see a "before" peek of the Herring River Estuary - with an incentive for us to return for an "after" look of the restoration on the environmental vitality of the Herring River Estuary.

The Herring Run in Middleboro, MA
As we paddled along the Herring River I recalled to my friends how, as a youngster, I used to visit the Herring Run on the Nemasket River in Middleboro, MA. Each spring, herring migrate from the ocean, up coastal rivers and into tributaries and lakes to spawn. The herring were so plentiful you felt you could walk

across their backs on the river – and so hundreds of people would come to see them.

Figure 197 - The Take-out

Friends and I would go to the fish ladders and catch herring with our hands and sell them to people. I remember coming home soaked and with coins in my pocket from selling my herring catch to people for food and garden fertilizer. It was a marvelous memory – and my connection to the Herring River Estuary.

Our paddle up the Herring River was well worth the expedition of nearly seven miles in five hours up and back on the Herring River Estuary:

- We saw Swans, Great Blue Heron, Osprey, Red Wing Blackbirds and other birds.

- Many times we thought we were at the end of the river and about to turn back, but we managed to find a path through the narrowing quagmire of brush, prickly bushes and marsh weeds.

- We passed under old wooden plank bridges

- We went through culverts under tar and dirt roads

- At about the three hours mark we found a road sign that told us we were passing the intersection of Bound Brook Island Road and the Atwood Higgins House.

Figure 198 - Bound Brook Isle Road

Day 2: Paddling the Mashpee River and Popponesset Bay

Figure 199 - Map Popponesset Bay

Day two's paddlers were Tim, Rob, John, Dundee and I.

- We put-in at Pirates Cove in Popponesset Bay.

- Paddled up the tidal Mashpee River. After an hour or so, we were in marsh weed, and decided to return to Popponesset Bay.

- Paddled around Popponesset Island. Beautiful homes and boats/yachts

- Lunch on the sandbar protecting Popponesset Bay

- Crossed Popponesset Bay to Pirates Cover in choppy water and wind

- Total paddling time about six hours

References:

- **Video and Blog:** Kayaking the Herring River Estuary and Popponesset Bay of Cape Cod http://outdooradventurers.blogspot.com/2013/10/kayaking-herring-river-estuary-of.html

- Friends of Herring River http://www.friendsofherringriver.org/

- Project Management associate Position Opening http://tiny.cc/6o584x

- Wellfleet's Herring River Tide Heights and Salinity Study http://tiny.cc/us584x

- Middleboro, Lakeville monitor herring run at Nemasket River - Raynham, MA (http://tiny.cc/79484x)

- Paddling in the Herring River Estuary: a nine minute video. http://tiny.cc/5f584x

- Design to aid kayakers, paddlers http://tiny.cc/iuqn6x

Winter

There are three kinds of people in this world. Those that watch things happen. Those that make things happen. And those that wonder what happened. Which kind are you? – Author Unknown

Snowshoeing in Bedford, NH at Benedictine Conservation and Van Loan Preserve

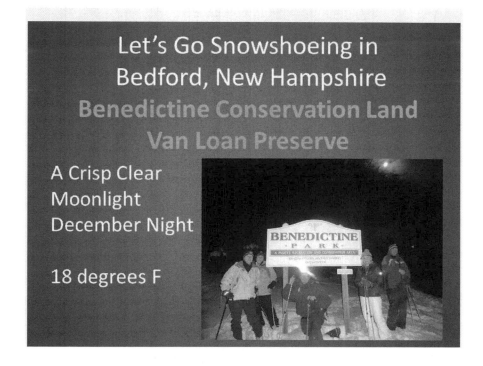

Figure 200 - A Bedford, NH Moonlight Snowshoe Hike

My friend Mark sent an email inviting his fellow outdoor enthusiasts to **a moonlight snowshoe** in the fields and woods of **Benedictine Conservation Land** and **Van Loan Preserve** in

Bedford, New Hampshire. Both areas are next to each other separated by Wallace Road.

These properties are protected by <u>The Bedford Land Trust</u> with conservation easements and allow public access to the trails for passive recreational use that remain in place forever. They were perfect for our snowshoeing quest.

Snowshoeing Benedictine Conservation Land

On a clear, moon lit night in December, nine (9) Outdoor Enthusiasts met at the <u>Benedictine Conservation Land</u> parking lot. The temperature was a mild 18 degrees F.

Figure 201 - Putting on Snowshoes with Headlamps

Figure 202 - Map Benedictine Park

Figure 203 - Benedictine Park Hikers

From the Kiosk leading to the Benedictine field we went clockwise on the Perimeter Trail climbing up the open field hill just inside the tree line. We completed the loop passing the Kiosk in about 15 minutes.

We then crossed Wallace Road to the woods of the **Van Loan Trail.**

Figure 204 - Van Loan Trail Sign

Van Loan Preserve

The **Van Loan Trail** is initially a narrow trail through the woods before crossing Riddle Brook Bridge. Thereafter the Van Loan

Trail reaches a junction whence we snowshoe onto the **Anna and Pic Loop** trail counterclockwise.

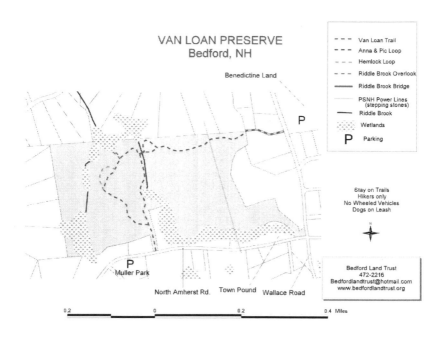

Figure 205 - Map Van Loan Preserve

The Anna and Pic Loop shortly returns to the Van Loan Trail from where we turn left back to the junction of the **Anna and Pic Loop.**

Figure 206 - Crossing Riddle Brook

We re-cross Riddle Brook Bridge following the Van Loan Trail to Wallace Road and the Benedictine Parking area.

Figure 207 - Rick and Steve at 5 degrees below zero

The total snowshoe trek was about an hour and forty-five minutes.

The videos below are generally dark because the only light was that of our headlamps and the light of the moon. I have left these videos dark to give you a sense of hiking in the dark led by shining headlamps and the voices of fellow snowshoers.

Figure 208 - The Gang of Hardy Snowshoers

It was a magnificent winter night. Wonderful friends. Beautiful, clean country air. Enjoy this short video of snow shoeing in Bedford, New Hampshire.

References
- Video and Blog: Snowshoeing in Bedford, NH at Benedictine Conservation and Van Loan Preserve http://tiny.cc/qoz26x
- Bedford Land Trust http://www.bedfordlandtrust.org/
- Benedictine Conservation Land http://tiny.cc/k0y26x

Re-using Outdoor Hand Warmers

I read a January 2015 Appalachian Mountain Club article on re-using outdoor hand warmers. Once exposed to air, the iron in the hand warmer package oxidizes and releases heat in the process - and you now have warm hands!

Therein lays the crucial piece of information. In order for the reaction to occur, the hand warmer needs a supply of oxygen. If you cut off the supply of oxygen, the chemical reaction ceases. And to cut off the oxygen, all you need to do is put the hand warmer in an air-tight zip-lock bag.

I decided to experiment with the content of this article. Not only did it work, BUT, I successfully used the same two hand warmers **two more times!**

Figure 209 - Re-Using Hand Warmers

Certainly there is money saving here, but a hand warmer is not a big expense – generally about $1 a pair. My message is that since hand warmers are capable of being reused you do not need to carry an excessive number of them. Just be sure to save the used hand warmer in an airlock bag.

I recommend keeping the unused packaged hand warmers as emergency spares.

Go to http://tiny.cc/kr2zux and read the AMC hand warmer article. To join or learn more about the **Appalachian Mountain Club** go to Outdoors.org/

Try this outdoor hand warmer experiment for yourself!

References
- **Video and Blog: Re-using Handwarmers http://outdooradventurers.blogspot.com/2015/03/re-using-outdoor-hand-warmers.html**
- See more **OutdoorSteve.com** tips at http://outdooradventurers.blogspot.com/

Winter in New Hampshire is more than Downhill Skiing

New Hampshire is known for its marvelous downhill skiing. Yes, we are very proud of this, BUT, there are many other winter outdoor happenings. Let me share some of the activities where my family and friends were participants, such as a sleigh ride in the great north woods of northern NH, cross-country skiing, a moonlight snowshoe hike and more.

Other times we are observers enjoying the excitement of watching ice climbers scale a mountain side of ice near Crawford Notch with views of the snow-capped 4,000 footers of the White Mountains Presidential range.

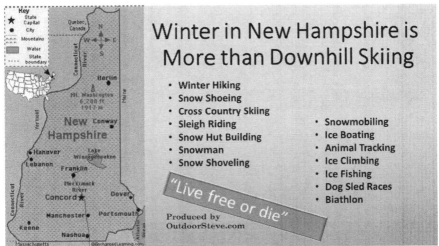

Figure 210 - Winter in NH is more than downhill skiing

The below blog has two videos. The top video is 12 minutes and gives **a taste of 14 NH winter happenings – all seen in the above list**. The bottom video is 41 minutes and is being shown by **Bedford Community Television (BCTV)**. I created the top video (12 mins) from key elements from the BCTV video.

Grab your favorite wintertime beverage, relax, and enjoy as Outdoor Steve presents his first-hand and personal insights of a multitude of New Hampshire winter activities.

Never say, "**I wish I had enjoyed winter in New Hampshire**".

Figure 211 - Crawford Notch Route 302

Figure 212 - Ice Climbing School at Crawford Notch

Figure 213 - Mt Washington Resort & Presidential Mountains

References

- **Video and Blog**: Winter in New Hampshire is more than downhill skiing http://outdooradventurers.blogspot.com/2015/02/winter-in-new-hampshire-is-more-than.html
- BCTV: Winter in New Hampshire is more than downhill skiing http://www.outdoorsteve.com
- http://outdooradventurers.blogspot.com/
- **Monson NH Center Ski Trip** -XC ski and snowshoeing for families **http://forestsocient.org/property/monson-center**

Ice Boating in New Hampshire

"Let's go ice boating!" It is a rare winter day in New Hampshire to have perfect ice boating conditions – meaning 2 inches or more of smooth ice with no snow coverage.

The temperature was 14 degrees. The ice had been frozen for the past month, and a few drilled holes showed the ice to be 8 – 10 inches thick – plenty of strength for ice boating – and smooth ice with no lingering snow.

Sailable ice is known in the sport as "hard water" versus sailing on liquid or "soft" water. Iceboats are strictly wind powered and need nearly snow-free smooth ice to sail.

The Homemade Iceboat

Dundee has many creative skills – and his iceboat reflects this.

Figure 214 - Dundee and His Handcrafted Iceboat

A Rare Opportunity

Ice boating can be a very unique experience. Once you get over the initial, "What am I doing here" feeling, you sense being one with the boat. You hear the wind in the sail and the rumble of the runners over the ice. Certainly at 14 degrees you must dress in layers for relative comfort.

Rare are the right ice boating conditions – sufficient ice – no snow – good wind – good weather – and not have to go to work! Smile.

Microspikes

Figure 215 - Microspikes – essential for walking on ice

The frequent crackling sound in the video is not the wind – it is the sound of microspikes as Steve walks on the ice. Microspikes offer serious traction on ice for walking and tasks such as pushing the iceboat.

See the below video and enjoy this unique experience – and even take an iceboat ride with Outdoor Steve.

Learn More About Dundee's Iceboat

Three 10" angle iron blades called "runners" support a triangular shaped wooden frame with a front steering tiller made from an old hockey stick. The blades are attached to the boat, one on each end of the rear cross plank and one at the fore end of the hull. The runner blade in the front is capable of rotation controlled by a tiller (the sawed off hockey stick). There is a backrest cushion seat in the middle for the driver.

Dundee drilled a sail posthole near the front of the boat. In the hole he positioned the mast from his summer "Sunfish" sail boat. (A Force 5 or Laser sailboat mast will work just as well.) A rope is tied to the sail and used by the driver to control the sail.

The boat with sail weighs about 150 lbs.

Starting, Steering and Stopping

The boat can be started by putting the boat sideways to the wind. You then pull onto the sail to capture the wind – and off you go.

The boat is steered with the hockey stick tiller to direct the front runner.

The driver pulls or releases the sail via the boom rope to angle the sail to catch the wind. The only seeming limitations to iceboat speed are windage, friction, the camber of the sail shape, strength of construction, quality of the ice surface, the level of skill, athleticism and fearlessness of the sailor. There are many styles of iceboats, but it is said, an iceboat of this style can go twice the speed of the wind, i.e., with a 20 knot breeze, your iceboat can reach a speed of nearly 40 MPH!

Tacking or coming about is a sailing maneuver by which a sailing vessel turns its bow into the wind through the 'no-go zone' so that the direction from which the wind blows changes from one side of the vessel to the other. The tacking method gets the iceboat up and down the pond. Catching the wind on an iceboat in the winter is exactly like sailing a sailboat in the summer.

Figure 216 - Ice Boating on Perkins Pond, Sunapee

References:
- **Video and Blog:** Ice Boating on Perkins Pond
  http://outdooradventurers.blogspot.com/2015/01/ice-boating-in-new-hampshire.html
- **Iceboat.org:** http://iceboat.org/faqiceboat.html
- **Tacking (sailing):**
  http://en.wikipedia.org/wiki/Tacking_%28sailing%29
- **Sailing:** http://en.wikipedia.org/wiki/Sailing
- Ice Boating in New Hampshire - Bedford Community TV
  http://tiny.cc/46y26x

An Eagle Sighting at Perkins Pond, New Hampshire

Figure 217 - An eagle on Perkins Pond

Four friends paddle on Perkins Pond in mid-April amongst open water and sheets of ice. They seek to determine if they can paddle from the northern point of the Pond at a spot called Chickadee Point to the southern section of the Pond noted as Piney Point. Is today going to be the day to declare ice-out?

Suddenly a large bird with a white head is spotted flying toward them. "Look an Eagle!"

Figure 218 - "Look – an eagle!"

References
- **Video and Blog:** An eagle has landed on Perkins Pond
  http://tiny.cc/cez26x

Other Winter Happenings at Perkins Pond
- Perkins Pond Ice-Out April 22, 2015 **http://tiny.cc/ihz26x**

- Ice boating in New Hampshire **http://tiny.cc/yiz26x**

- Winter in New Hampshire is More Thank Downhill Skiing **http://tiny.cc/rjz26x**

- Re-using Outdoor Hand Warmers **http://tiny.cc/wkz26x**

Perkins Pond Ice-Out April 22, 2015

Figure 219 - Perkins Pond Logo

Perkins Pond Protective Association (PPPA)

On March 1, 2015 Perkins Pond had 18 plus inches of ice. The ice was insulated with hard packed snow from snowmobiles and XC skiers and what was left of the ten feet of winter snow. Would the winter ever end? Would the ice ever melt?

Gary, President of the Perkins Protective Association, in collaboration with Dundee, came up with the idea of getting Perkins Ponders thinking toward spring and gathering money for the Association's water monitoring efforts with a Perkins Pond Ice-Out Contest.

Gary sent a March 18 email to all homeowners registered with the Association announcing the Perkins Pond Ice-Out Contest. All submissions had to be in by March 26, 2015.

Dundee was asked to set the criteria for ice-out. Steve was asked to monitor the official occurrence of "ice-out", along with Gary.

Ice-out is deemed to have occurred when a boat can freely navigate from the point separating the coves at the south end of the pond known as "Piney Point" to the point at the north end of the pond marking the entrance to the outlet known as "Chickadee Point."

On April 17, there was some open water around the north edges of the pond, and Dundee, Gary and Steve slid their canoe and two kayaks into the open water and proceeded to Chickadee Point (next to the outlet by the large beaver lodge). Their efforts to paddle south to Piney Point (the peninsula at the south end of the pond) were quickly stifled as the ice was too thick for a canoe or kayak to penetrate.

To inform those Perkins Ponders interested in the ice-out progress, Ann and Robert generously let us share their web link to their live web cams showing views from the north end of the pond to the south end. This allowed those with Internet access to view the ice-out evolution 24 hours a day.

On Apr 18th Steve paddled from Chickadee point to the public landing when he could go no further due to the ice.

On Sunday April 19th, Dundee, Gary, Mike D., Gerry and Steve attempted to paddle from Chickadee Point to Piney Point but were prevented by the remaining ice sheet.

From April 20 – 21 Gary and Dundee continued monitoring ice-out from Chickadee Point to Piney Point.

On April 22 in the late afternoon Gary took pictures of ice-out on Perkins Pond.

Throughout ice-out Mike G. had his live web cam viewing from South to North. Further, Mike G. condensed the April 20 - 22 video of ice-out to a 90 second movie clip which you will see on the video here. This is a fascinating condensed view of the last three days of ice on Perkins Pond.

Figure 220 - Check those Eagle Talons

As an added benefit to ice-out, on April 19th the monitors spotted an eagle landing on an ice flow in front of Mike D.'s house. Steve managed to film the eagle – and this exciting occasion is included in the video.

Enjoy the below video of the ice-out monitoring from April 17 to April 22.

PERKINS POND ICE-OUT CONTEST

OFFICIAL RULES AND REGULATIONS

ICE-OUT IS DEEMED TO HAVE OCCURRED WHEN A BOAT CAN FREELY NAVIGATE FROM THE POINT SEPARATING THE TWO COVES AT THE SOUTH END OF THE POND, KNOWN AS "PINEY POINT", TO THE POINT AT THE NORTH END OF THE POND MARKING THE ENTRANCE TO THE OUTLET, KNOWN AS "CHICKADEE POINT".

THE CONTEST WILL BE A TRADITIONAL 50/50 FORMAT WITH THE WINNER RECEIVING 1/2 OF THE "KITTY" AND THE OTHER 1/2 GOING TO THE PERKINS POND PROTECTIVE ASSOCIATION'S GENERAL FUND TO ASSIST IN ASSOCIATION ANNUAL ACTIVITIES.

THE WINNER WILL BE THE PERSON WITH THE PREDICTION THAT IS CLOSEST TO THE EXACT DAY OF ICE-OUT.

IN THE EVENT MORE THAN ONE PERSON PREDICTS THE EXACT DATE OF ICE-OUT, THE 50/50 KITTY WILL BE SPLIT EVENLY BETWEEN THE WINNERS.

DUNDEE WILL BE RESPONSIBLE FOR DETERMINING WHEN THE CRITERIA HAS BEEN MET FOR OFFICIAL ICE-OUT.

STEVE WILL ACT AS MONITOR TO ENSURE THE CRITERIA FOR ICE-OUT HAS BEEN MET.

YOU MUST BE AT LEAST 18 YEARS OF AGE TO PARTICIPATE IN THE CONTEST.

ALL ENTRIES MUST BE RECEIVED NO LATER THAN MIDNIGHT ON MARCH 25TH, 2015.

ENTRIES ARE $5.00 EACH WITH A LIMIT OF 10 ENTRIES PER PERSON.

Other Winter Happenings at Perkins Pond

- 2015 Perkins Pond Eagle Sighting

- Ice boating in New Hampshire

- Winter in New Hampshire is More Thank Downhill Skiing

- Re-using Outdoor Hand Warmers

Perkins Pond Ice-out Dates Recorded by Dundee and Linda		
	March	April
1993		18
1994		20
1995	29	
1996		12
1997		10
1998		19
1999		7
2000	28	
2001		28
2002		1
2003		21
2004		13
2005		12
2006	31	
2007		23
2008		20
2009		5
2010		1
2011		20
2012	18	
2013		10
2014		19
2015		**22**

Figure 221 - Perkins Pond Ice-out Dates 1993-2015

References

- **Video and Blog:** Ice Out on Perkins Pond
  http://tiny.cc/jw984x

Winter Hike - Carter Notch Hut on Appalachian Trail

My friend John called and asked me to join him on a winter hike into Carter Notch Hut. John's son Ryan would be hiking with a friend and John wanted to meet them at their overnight stay at the Appalachian Mountain Club hut located on the Appalachian Trail. John and I are life-long members of the AMC.

Mount Hedgehog – a warm-up hike

Figure 222 - Which Way to Mt Hedgehog?

To prepare for this 3.8 mile hike into the winter wilds of the snowy and icy White Mountains, John wanted to go to the White Mountain area a day earlier for a day hike.

On Friday morning we were at the Kancamagus Highway trailhead for the Mount Hedgehog (2520 ft.) loop trail.

The five mile loop trail was moderately difficult, meaning upward switchback trails, crossing small brooks, over and under a few downed trees across the trail, and a reasonable grade with only the final sections a bit steep and requiring climbing up and over granite ledges.

The AMC trail guidebook suggested this hike could be done in three hours. We did the loop in a respectable three and a half hours. We paced ourselves stopping every fifteen minutes or so to drink water and chew trail mix. As we approached the top, wind and cold caused me to don my winter gloves. We paused at the top for magnificent views of Mt. Passaconaway, the Presidential range and Mt Chocorua (see more on Mt Chocorua in the Summer section of this book).

Figure 223 - Can you see the Squalls of Snow Below Us?
Looking down from the peak over the tree-studded valley and north toward Mt Washington, we saw dark clouds blowing our way with squalls of snow beneath them – and we quickly picked up our pace, not wanting to be caught on the top of the mountain. John took this picture from the top of Hedgehog and you can see

the fast moving snow squall as a white-looking cloud spiraling to the ground in the valley and quickly heading our way.

The loop back to the trailhead was steep from the top and I could feel my quads aching. All in all, Mt Hedgehog was a good day hike and certainly helped prepare us for the next day's four mile hike into Carter Notch Hut.

Carter Notch Hut

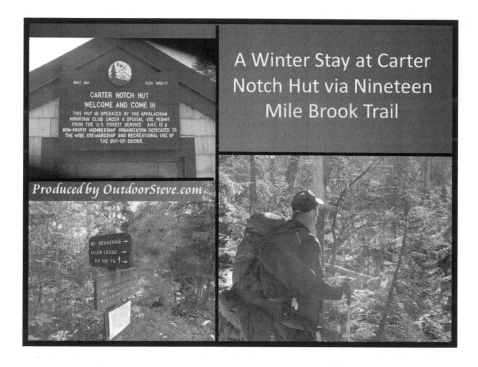

Figure 224 - Carter Hut via Nineteen Mile Brook Trail

Carter Notch Hut, elevation 3,450 feet, is the most eastern of the eight AMC huts in NH. In winter the hut is self-service, meaning a caretaker stokes the wood stove at the hut from 5 pm until 9:30 pm (unless extreme cold dictates otherwise). Self-service includes self-cooking and hikers bring their own food and use the hut's utensils and gas stove for cooking.

Water Carried to Hut from Lake

Figure 225 - Drinking Water from Pond for Boiling

There is no running water inside Carter Notch hut in winter, but water is carried into the hut in five gallon jugs as needed for potable water (after boiling). Hikers share responsibility for getting the water through a hole in the ice from a lake near the hut.

Two bunk houses are separate from the hut, and are unheated. The bunkhouses essentially provide bunk beds and protection from rain, snow and wind. Temperatures may reach way below zero in the depth of winter, so a winter sleeping bag is advisable, if not mandatory, such as one rated to -20 degrees F and preferably even lower.

The Master Maine Guide I have often traveled with in summer adventures uses a bag rated for 35 degrees below zero whenever he ventures out into the North Maine Woods during the winter months on guided 5 day cross-country ski trips across Maine's Baxter State Park. Staying warm during the night makes your outing much more enjoyable. Being cold during the night not only saps your energy, but leaves a bad taste in your mouth for ever getting out and enjoying those special scenic vistas and quiet solitudes that only a visit in winter can provide.

Figure 226 - Trekking Poles for balance and backpacks

John and I used trekking poles to reach the hut, which were important for balance and saving our knees as we poled and stepped over and up on ice covered boulders. As we neared the Hut, the snow began to get deeper, maybe a foot or so in depth.

Figure 227 - John Crossed Over the Ice/Snow Plank Bridge

We crossed four wooden planked bridges of which one had obviously been washed out, most likely in last month's northern NH flood, and in its place was an eight inch ice covered plank. You will see our balancing acts in the video as we warily crisscross three to four feet above the waters of Nineteen Mile Brook and the mountain run-offs.

The Hut Experience

Very few people remain strangers at a wilderness hut. A winter hike to a hut offers a bond to each person there. We all got to the hut the same way, on foot.

Hut life offers a common denominator for camaraderie and a "Where are you from?" opener to sharing stories, asking strangers, now friends, to join a card game, and learning new games memorable to hut experience. Ryan taught us a game new to us, "Pass the Pigs" – and soon we had an exciting game going.

We shared conversation with hikers from Littleton, NH, Maine, and Canada. "He who passes through these doors are strangers no more".

For dinner that night at the Hut, John made a delicious entrée of chicken potpie. Ryan made an apple crisp that was to die for! The next morning's breakfast was at the hands of John with bacon and eggs enjoyed with hot coffee and chocolate to prepare us for the hike out.

Ryan and Peter decided to hike the Carter Dome and Mount Height trail back to the trailhead. This is a strenuous hike, but the rewards are magnificent views from the barren peaks of four-thousand footers. John and I returned via Nineteen Mile Brook Trail with a bit of regret for not bringing our crampons. John and I took the Nineteen Mile Brook Trail back to the Trailhead on Route 16.

Enjoy the video as John and I never have to say, "We wish we had spent a winter night at AMC's Carter Notch Hut."

Video of Hike to Carter Notch Hut
• **Blog: A Winter Hike to Carter Notch Hut**   http://outdooradventurers.blogspot.com/2011/11/winter-hike-to-carter-notch-hut-on.html   • **Video of Visit to Carter Notch Hut via Nineteen-mile Trail**   http://www.youtube.com/watch?feature=player_embedded&v=kd8JaqvVUfMotch Hutch

Training for Winter Wild in New Hampshire

Winter in New Hampshire offers unique and exciting opportunities for outdoor enthusiasts. In this month's blog I share my training and research in preparation for running a race up the ski slopes of Mt Sunapee in the middle of the winter. The race is called "Winter Wild" (http://www.winterwild.com/) and is held in March at Mt Sunapee Ski Mountain, Newbury, NH (http://www.mountsunapee.com/).

The rules for this race are pretty simple. Whatever you carry up the hill is what you must descend the hill with. You cannot leave anything stashed anywhere on the mountain! Whatever you go up with, you must return with to the bottom of the hill. Acceptable devices are downhill skis, XC Skis, Telemark Skis, snowboards, snowshoes, crampons or just plain running shoes.

Figure 228 - Pats Peak Ski Trail Map with Winter Wild Course

The first **Video Reference** below describes my winter training run at Pats Peak (http://www.patspeak.com/). The second video is my practice run on the Mt Sunapee course – one week before the race.

Both courses are marked on the video's maps in red and follow the perimeter of their ski areas. The courses start at the bottom of the mountain at the ski lodges, and finish on steep downhills that rush you back to the lodge. The Pats Peak course is counter clockwise, and the Mt Sunapee course is clockwise.

The Mt Sunapee course starts up Elliot Slope to the access road where you begin ascending the Williamson Trail to Stovepipe and up to the Mount Sunapee summit. You descend the Upper Ridge trail all the way down to the Lower Ridge trail and finish in front of the Spruce Lodge.

The learning experience:
Since this was be my first time doing this type of winter event, my practice runs at both Pat's Peak and Mt Sunapee would help me decide:

- Was I in good enough physical shape to do my first ever uphill and downhill ski run?

- Do I wear running shoes or hiking boots? Or, do I carry my back country skis up the hill, and ski down? Or do I carry my snowshoes uphill and use them downhill?

- Do I wear crampons? I had never run in crampons before so I was concerned about their feel.

- What clothing should I wear for a run up a mountain in a New Hampshire winter at below freezing temps?

- After the Pats Peak run, I experienced a sore right calf. My remedy was to use a wooden dowel to massage my calf on the days before the race. Would my calf stand up under race conditions?

- During my Mt Sunapee training run, I was half way

through the two mile downhill when I felt an ache in my quads. I walked for a minute and then continued my run. That evening I started using my wooden dowel to massage both quads. Was I really ready for Mt Sunapee?

- The Sunapee training run also produced a blister on my left middle toe. I suspect the uphill trek in my hiking boots caused this. Would a Band-Aid two days before the race be enough to cure the blister?

- In preparation for this grueling uphill/downhill run, I began, two days before the race, to drink lots of water as a preventive for possible cramps. Did I start my hydration soon enough?

- Did my running base of twenty to twenty five miles a week have me at a good cardiac level for this unique winter ski mountain run? The lesson here, is before you do a ski mountain race, be sure to get in good physical shape.

The section after this, **Winter Wild at Mount Sunapee New Hampshire,** describes the day of the race results.

Enjoy the below videos for this unique winter event, and never have to say, "I wish I had run the Mt Sunapee Winter Wild race".

Video Reference Winter Wild in New Hampshire
- **Blog: Mt Sunapee and Pat's Peak Winter Wild** http://outdooradventurers.blogspot.com/2011/02/winter-wild-in-new-hampshire.html
- **Pat's Peak** http://www.youtube.com/watch?feature=player_embedded&v=wCzj8hWdbuI
- **Mt Sunapee** http://www.youtube.com/watch?feature=player_embedded&v=G4n_NgzyF8g

Winter Wild at Mt Sunapee New Hampshire

Winter in New Hampshire offers exciting opportunities for outdoor enthusiasts. The **Winter Wild** is a unique ski area race (http://www.winterwild.com/) and is held at Mt Sunapee Ski Mountain, Newbury, NH (http://www.mountsunapee.com/).

The section prior to this, **Training for Winter Wild**, describes the training and concerns I had with preparing for the **Winter Wild at Sunapee.** Fitness level, type of skiing equipment, injuries, and other concerns are shared. If you have a desire to experience an exceptional NH winter challenge, be sure to be prepared both physically and mentally.

The rules for this four mile snow-covered uphill/downhill race at Mt Sunapee are pretty easy. You cannot leave anything stashed anywhere on the mountain! Whatever you go up with you must return with to the bottom of the hill.

Oh, did I mention the temperature was ten degrees with a slight "cooling" breeze?

The 133 athletes wore a mixture of ski attire and their warmest winter running clothing. Some wore their alpine, telemark, or cross-country skis and did a combination of skiing with mostly herringbone "walking" up the steep ski slopes with the expectation they were going to reach the top and go "screaming" down on those same skis. Others backpacked their skis to the top. Many skiers used climbing "skins" on the bottom of their skis for traction uphill on the icy and snowy slopes. Quite a few wore crampons on their hiking boots or running shoes.

My choice was my hiking boots with my ice crampons.

The Mt Sunapee course is marked on the map in red and follows the clockwise perimeter of the ski area. The course begins at Spruce Lodge and then proceeds up Elliot Slope to the access road where you ascend the Williamson Trail to Stovepipe and on up to the Mount Sunapee summit. You descend the Upper Ridge trail to the Lower Ridge trail returning to the lodge.

Figure 229 - Mount Sunapee Trail Map & Winter Wild Course

Some Winter Wild moments:
• We had a 6:30 am start in order to have all the participants off the mountain by the time the Mountain opens at 8 am for the general public.
• Halfway through the two-mile uphill, I felt a cramp coming on in my right calf. I slowed to a walk until I felt the cramp was not returning, and then continued my run and walk pace.
• It was foggy as the athletes ascended the 2,726 foot mountain with its three secondary peaks - and at the uppermost peak it was snowing hard. The temperature at the top was in the mid-teens.

Enjoy **Video References** as you join me in this unique winter event.

Oh, I had an enjoyable run. I was thrilled to have participated in this unique winter race.

I never have to say, "I wish I had run the Mt Sunapee Winter Wild race".

Video Reference Mt Sunapee Winter Wild Race
• Blog: Mt Sunapee Winter Wild
http://outdooradventurers.blogspot.com/2011/03/winter-wild-at-mt-sunapee-new-hampshire.html
• Mt Sunapee Winter Wild
http://www.youtube.com/watch?feature=player_embedded&v=1jQpVHUg3q0

A Winter Sleigh Ride

One winter on a snowy February day at Dixville Notch, New Hampshire, I had the pleasure to interview sleigh ride owners Dennis and Tina Willey (hitchhorses.com). The Willeys took Cathy and I "over hill and over dale" on a romantic sleigh ride at The Balsams Grand Resort wooded property.

Figure 230 - A Sleigh in the North Country of NH

Figure 231 - North Country Cross-Country Ski Trail

See the below **Video Reference** and **Never say, "I wish I had enjoyed unique winter experiences in New Hampshire".**

Video Reference A Winter Sleigh Ride
• Blog: A Unique New Hampshire Winter http://outdooradventurers.blogspot.com/2011/02/enjoy-winter-experience-in-new.html
• XC Skiing in Bedford, NH http://www.youtube.com/watch?feature=player_embedded&v=zhtnvjLhq-A
• Enjoy a Winter Sleigh Ride http://www.youtube.com/watch?feature=player_embedded&v=zu9z3dVaiYk

The Outdoors as a Daily Component of Life

Regret for the things we did can be tempered by time. It is the things we did not do that is inconsolable – Sydney J. Harris

Outdoor Enthusiast Campfire Chat: How to Cook an Egg in an Onion

A Great North Woods paddling and tenting trip to northern New Hampshire's Lake Francis allowed me to take my campsite breakfast cooking experience a bit further. Paul Tawrell's outdoor enthusiast book, **Wilderness Camping and Hiking**, described a method of cooking an egg over an open campfire in an onion. Being one to never say, "I wish I had cooked an egg in an onion over an open campfire", I decided to try Paul's recommendation.

Figure 232 - Egg in an Onion Cooked in Campfire Ashes

Figure 233 - The First Taste of Egg Cooked in an Onion

Figure 234 - The Egg is Eaten!

Appreciate the below **Video Reference Egg in an Onion** to see Outdoor Steve's experience with an onion, egg, and campfire.

This video has gone viral on YouTube.com and as of the date of this book there have been over 50,000 views of Cook an Egg in an Onion Over an Open Campfire by Outdoor Steve.wmv. http://tiny.cc/9tb94x.

References: Campside Chats
- **Blog: How Cook an Egg in an Onion**
  http://outdooradventurers.blogspot.com/2010/06/outdoor-enthusiast-happenings-how-to.html

- **Cook an Egg in an Onion Over an Open Campfire**
  http://www.youtube.com/watch?feature=player_embedded&v=fkg9tenysmM
- **Using an Orange to Cook an Egg**
  http://www.youtube.com/watch?feature=player_embedded&v=7HTqcR2ep4U
- **Starting Your Campfire with Rotten Birch Bark**
  http://www.youtube.com/watch?feature=player_embedded&v=sEjxuiHX5vs

Outdoor Enthusiast Campfire Chat: How to Cook an Egg in an Orange & How to Make a Banana Sundae

John is not only an avid outdoor enthusiast; he also is an excellent camp cook. He usually assumes responsibility to plan and cook our meals for our outdoor treks. He expressed a desire to "do something different" on this trip. Through a Google search he found a site recommending cooking an egg inside an orange over an open campfire. The result was absolutely delicious. Go to the **References** below to see a video of this unique breakfast treat.

Figure 235 - Cook an Egg in an Orange

John further impressed us with his campfire cooking creativity by serving us a banana sundae – a banana with most of the skin left on it. Slice the banana lengthwise, and then put bits of chocolate in the slit. Place the combined desert inside aluminum foil and heat in the campfire ashes for a few minutes. Indeed, it tastes like a banana sundae!

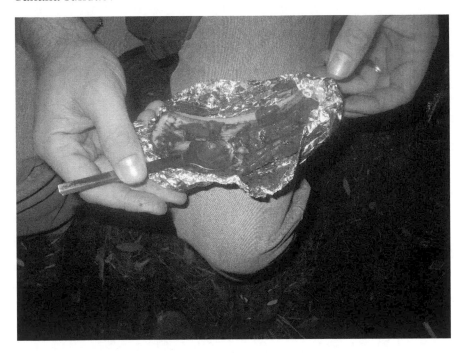

Figure 236 - Banana Sundae Prepared on Open Flame

- How to cook an egg in an orange over an open campfire
  https://www.youtube.com/watch?v=7HTqcR2ep4U&fea
  ture=player_embedded

- Blog: How to cook an egg in an onion
  http://outdooradventurers.blogspot.com/2010/06/outdoo
  r-enthusiast-happenings-how-to.html

A Hand-crafted Ladder from a Beaver Fell

Enjoy the below **Video Reference** describing the process of making a very unique hand-crafted ladder from a beaver fell hemlock tree taken from the north end of New Hampshire's Perkins Pond. A "beaver fell" is a fallen tree gnawed through by a beaver. Notice the end of the hemlock looks like it was axed by a human, BUT indeed it was gnawed through by a beaver

Beavers love to eat the bark and leaves from the trees that they fell. Their favorite trees are aspens but they will also eat birch, alder, willow, and mountain maple. They usually prefer trees between 2-6 inches in diameter. A busy beaver can chew through a 5 inch willow tree in 3 minutes! With the leftover wood they create dams and lodges. A pair of beavers takes down about 400 trees per year. (http://www.wildernessclassroom.com/wilderness-library/beaver/)

Figure 237 - A Beaver Fell Hemlock

Figure 238 - Craftsman's Work from a Beaver Fell

- **Video Reference for a Hand-Crafted Ladder from a Beaver Fell**
  http://youtu.be/uwpElEsRq3E
- http://www.wildernessclassroom.com/wilderness-library/beaver/

Eclectic Sharing

Don't judge those who try and fail, judge those who fail to try. – Unknown

Community Emergency Response Team (CERT) Search and Rescue Training

Community Emergency Response Team (CERT) is your neighbors, friends, and co-workers - a collection of community volunteers that want themselves and their town to be prepared in the event of an emergency or disaster.

I am a member of Bedford, NH CERT and the Londonderry, NH ALERT (**A** **L**ondonderry **E**mergency **R**esponse **T**eam). Their missions are the same in maintaining a trained, dedicated group of volunteers:
1) Assist their communities and its public safety departments in times of need.
2) Serve as a community source for education on emergency preparedness and prevention.
3) Recruit and regularly train volunteer citizens.

Search and Rescue Training (SAR)
I have taken advantage of search and rescue training offered by both the Londonderry ALERT and Bedford CERT teams. The types of their search and rescue training I have been part of include:

- Wilderness line search to locate missing persons or objects (SAR).
- Orienteering – how to read and use a compass and/or map.
- Red Cross Advanced First Aid certification including CPR, splints, bandaging and moving patients.
- Amateur Radio (Ham Radio Operators)

Below are briefs of selected CERT and ALERT training exercises, which blend the above learned skills for SAR, map and compass, first aid, and ham radio communication.

Line Search and Rescue Training at Musquash Conservation Area, Londonderry, NH

Figure 239 - Searchers Prepare for a Winter Line Search

Under the general name of Line Search and Rescue training, the ALERT and CERT teams teach and practice four general steps:

1. **Locate the victim using Line Search Method:** Maintain a line of searchers arms-length apart. Walk straight ahead (as best in a wilderness environment). A person behind the line guides the line to maintain a straight line of search. Left and right end line searchers insure line is staying together. Move through assigned search area looking for signs of distress or hint of missing person or item. See **Figure 231 Searchers Prepared for a Winter Line Search**.
2. **Access the victim**.
3. **Stabilize the victim** by treating any life threatening injuries.

4. **Transport the victim** to a safe area for professional assessment.

There is a safety dress inspection to be sure all line searchers are dressed appropriately for the condition of the environment. If someone is unequipped they cannot participate. For example, in winter weather a check is made to insure no cotton clothing is worn. No jeans are allowed. Best fabrics are polypropylene, silk or wicking fabrics on the skin layer. Then layers of wool and fleece. Proper footwear, hydration and a snack are needed for an extensive excursion. No sneakers or sandals allowed.

For this exercise a body (dummy) is placed within an area and the line search team assigned a section. When the dummy is found, the team proceeds to provide first aid and then transports the "person" to a safe area.

Figure 240 - First Aid Administered On-site

Training was at the Hickory Hill Road trailhead of the Musquash conservation area off High Range Rd. in Londonderry.

Map of Musquash Trails, Londonderry, NH
http://tiny.cc/iyd75x

Orienteering Training by Londonderry NH ALERT at Beaver Brook Association, Hollis, NH

Figure 241 - Getting a Compass Bearing

There is a Beaver Brook Orienteering Course laid out among the trails where we can apply map and compass skills and off trail navigation. Each attendee must bring their own compass and a GPS device (if they have a GPS), and print a copy of the trail maps and orienteering course. http://www.beaverbrook.org/wp-content/uploads/2011/05/Beaver-Brook-Seasonal-0907-map.pdf .

The Londonderry ALERT conducted the training. We combined hiking with a few hours of navigation training with map and compass. We practiced how to read a map, determine a compass bearing, and how to follow that bearing to 9 different points identified on the orienteering map.

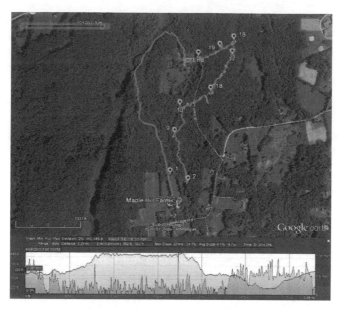

Figure 242 - Our Beaver Brook Association GPS Route

Amateur Radio – Ham Radio Operators

Both CERT and ALERT offer instruction in using hand operated radios. Members practice their radio skills in the SAR exercises. Ham operators have in common a basic knowledge

of radio technology, operating principles and regulations, demonstrated

Figure 243 - Ham Radio

by passing an examination for a license to operate on radio frequencies known as the "Amateur Bands." These frequencies are allocated by the Federal Communications Commission for use by hams from just above the AM broadcast band all the way up into extremely high microwave frequencies.

Learn more about Amateur Radio at **New Hampshire American Radio Relay League Section Web Site** http://www.arrl-nh.org/

Map and Compass Training

The UNH Cooperative Extension, provided a two hour class on compass and topographical maps. The presenter emphasized Map, Compass and Pacing, so, "you will know where you are."

Pacing: We began the class by going outdoors. The instructor used a measuring tape to lay out a 100 foot distance, and had each member of the class count their normal paces back and forth to get the average number of steps. He wanted us to "memorize forever", that, in my case, 40 paces closely approximates 100 feet. *The Lesson: In the woods with a map, knowing distance can be critical.*

Maps: Here are a few map items discussed:
- Go to the Internet and you can get both a map and an aerial .photo (e.g. https://www.google.com/maps
- You can also get topographical maps on the Internet
  - http://topomaps.usgs.gov/
  - http://www.digital-topo-maps.com/
- **Understand how to read topographical maps http://tiny.cc/49c75x**

Compass tips:
- Declination – in New Hampshire, magnetic North is 16 degrees west from true North. Declination is zero degrees on the west side of the Great Lakes
- The compass arrow is ALWAYS correct!
- Box the arrow - aligning the compass needle north
- You can see about 100 feet in the woods of New Hampshire. Sight on a rock or a tree.
- Good to know measures:
  - 1 mile is 5,280 feet
  - 1 acre is 43,560 sq. ft. or approximately 208' x 208'

Compass and Map References (One Page Briefs from Appalachian Mountain Club):
- **How to Choose a Compass http://tiny.cc/bwt75x**
- **Don't Get Lost: Finding your way there and back http://tiny.cc/put75x**
- **How to read topographical maps http://tiny.cc/2xt75x**

Figure 244 - SAR Bedford CERT & Londonderry ALERT

References:

- **Too learn more about Bedford CERT**
  http://www.bedfordnhcert.org/
- **To learn more about Londonderry ALERT**
  http://www.londonderryalert.org/
- http://www.extension.unh.edu
- **Map of Musquash Trails, Londonderry, NH**
  http://tiny.cc/iyd75x
- **Beaver Brook Association Orienteering Map**
  http://tiny.cc/s0c75x
- **Beaver Brook Association Trail Map**
  http://tiny.cc/g4c75x
- **New Hampshire American Radio Relay League Section**
  Web Site http://www.arrl-nh.org/

CERT Net Control Training on Search and Rescue (SAR)

The Bedford, New Hampshire Community Emergency Response Team (CERT) (http://www.bedfordnhcert.org) includes members trained as ham radio operators. To be a ham radio operator a person must pass an Amateur License exam conducted by the Federal Communications Commission Universal Licensing System. Upon passing the Operator Technician exam a person receives their unique call sign, such as KC1BJI.

Figure 245 - Hand Held Radio

An **amateur radio net**, or simply **ham net**, is an "on-the-air" gathering of amateur radio operators. Most nets convene on a regular schedule and specific frequency, and are organized for a particular purpose, such as the Bedford CERT hams use a directed net to maintain and practice their radio communication skills. A formal, or *directed* net, has a single *net control station* (NCS) that manages its operation for a given session. The NCS operator calls the net to order at its designated start time, periodically calls for participants to join, listens for them to answer (or *check in*) keeps track of the roster of stations for that particular net session, and generally orchestrates the operation of the net.

I was the NCS person under the tutelage of Ric, Communications Officer of Bedford CERT.

Each week's agenda has a check-in with each person using their Federal Communication Commission assigned call sign. They also identify the type of power used (such as fixed station commercial power, fixed station emergency power, mobile or Handheld). Announcements and training education are part of this exercise. The announcements are items of interest to the CERT members (for example upcoming CERT training sessions and meetings).

Tonight's training session was conducted by Steve. The training focused on two related search and rescue (SAR) topics of particular importance in rural New Hampshire:

- **The Hiker Responsibility Code**

- **Ten Essentials of Hiking**

The **Hiker Responsibility Code,** was developed in 2003 as a joint program between the White Mountain National Forest (WMNF) and the New Hampshire Fish and Game Department (NHFG). The Hiker Responsibility Code was needed when the number of WMNF search and rescue occurrences were increasing because of negligence and ignorance on the part of wilderness hikers. The costs of air searches and rescues, along with the safety risk to SAR volunteers, were unacceptable.

The Hiker responsibility code is intended to ensure that hikers are equipped with the gear, knowledge and experience they need to have a safe journey into the wilderness.

Knowing the **Hiker Responsibility Code** and the essential equipment and knowledge (**Ten Essentials of Hiking**) may save your life in the wilderness, it could also save you being charged thousands of dollars for YOUR search and rescue. The New Hampshire Fish and Game Department is authorized to sell voluntary Hike Safe Cards for $25 per person and $35 per family. People who obtain the cards are not liable to repay rescue costs if they need to be rescued due to negligence on their part in the wilderness. The card is valuable for anyone hiking, paddling, cross country skiing or engaging in other outdoor recreation. An individual may still be liable for response expenses if they are deemed to have recklessly or to have intentionally created a situation requiring an emergency response.

People who possess a current New Hampshire Fish and Game hunting or fishing license, or a current registration for an off-highway recreational vehicle, snowmobile or boat, are already exempt from repaying rescue costs due to negligence.

Follow the Hiker Responsibility Code
(http://hikesafe.com/)
You are responsible for yourself, so **be prepared:**

- **With knowledge and gear.** Become self-reliant by learning about the terrain, conditions, local weather and your equipment before you start.

- **To leave your plans.** Tell someone where you are going, the trails you are hiking, when you will return and your emergency plans.

- **To stay together.** When you start as a group, hike as a group, end as a group. Pace your hike to the slowest person.

- **To turn back.** Weather changes quickly in the mountains. Fatigue and unexpected conditions can also affect your hike. Know your limitations and when to postpone your hike. The mountains will be there another day.

- **For emergencies**. Even if you are headed out for just an hour, an injury, severe weather or a wrong turn could become life threatening. Don't assume you will be rescued; know how to rescue yourself.

- **To share the hiker code with others.**

Voluntary **Hike Safe cards** are available at http://www.wildlife.state.nh.us/safe/index.html.

Figure 246 - Hike Safe – It's Your Responsibility

Ten + 2 Essentials when Hiking
http://www.outdoors.org/recreation/hiking/hiking-gear.cfm
1. **Map**
2. **Compass**
3. **Warm Clothing**
4. **Extra Food and Water**
5. **Flashlight or headlamp**
6. **Matches/fire starters**
7. **First aid kit/repair kit**
8. **Whistle**
9. **Rain/wind gear**
10. **Pocket knife**
11. **Contractor type 40- gallon trash bags**
12. **Duct tape**

Notice the above **Ten + 2**. Most discussions deal with the ten essentials to carry, but personally, I also carry two trash bags and duct tape.

The below two White Mountain National Forest signs say it all when it comes to relating the **Hiker Responsibility Code** and the **Ten Essentials**.

Figure 247 - Signs to Hike Safe say it all

For those interested in more Search and Rescue information, see my Blog post **Community Emergency Response Team (CERT) Search and Rescue Training** http://tiny.cc/wa8e7x).

References

1. **For more information on Bedford NH CERT**
   http://www.bedfordnhcert.org

2. **Blog: Community Emergency Response Team (CERT) Search and Rescue Training** http://tiny.cc/wa8e7x

3. **Follow the Hiker Responsibility Code**
   (http://hikesafe.com/)

4. **Ten Essentials of Hiking**
   http://www.outdoors.org/recreation/hiking/hiking-gear.cfm

5. **New Hampshire Fish and Game Department (NHFG)**
   http://www.wildlife.state.nh.us/safe/index.html

6. **Federal Communications Commission Universal Licensing System**
   http://wireless.fcc.gov/uls/index.htm?job=home

7. **Amateur Radio Net**
   https://en.wikipedia.org/wiki/Amateur_radio_net

Dreaming the Appalachian Trail

The Man - Brad Viles

Figure 248 - Brad Viles: Dreaming the Appalachian Trail

I encourage you to read Brad Viles's book, Dreaming the Appalachian Trail. I write this blog in admiration of a man I have met in person only once. We have corresponded via email, have chatted on the phone, and have exchanged books. Indeed, I have read many of his writings in the **Bangor Daily News**. Brad was a weekly freelance writer for this Maine newspaper with articles focused on the great outdoors from a person who made the outdoors a daily component of his life.

I was so enthralled with **Dreaming ...** that I just had to have my wife Cathy listen as I read her two chapters of beautiful prose that reminded me of reading Robert Frost's, *"Two roads diverged in* *the woods, and I took the one less traveled by"*. I pictured Brad reading to an intent group of outdoor enthusiasts by a campfire next to a river in Maine.

Snippets from Contents of Dreaming

Dreaming the Appalachian Trail is a fictional account of Brad's Appalachian Trail (AT) hike from Georgia to Maine. Along the way he encounters violent storms, strange people, spectacular scenery and events that change his life. The trail itself is a major character in this story of imagination and wonder.

I absolutely loved the **Dreaming the AT** characters, and in particular, Non-stop's frog/tadpole metaphor. *"A frog can't explain to a tadpole what he will become when grown. The tadpole can't understand about having legs, no tail and breathing air, even though a frog is exactly what the tadpole would become when it's an adult. I could not express to anyone what it was like to walk over two thousand miles, so I was a frog, surrounded by tadpoles."*

Gosh, I read that comparison and immediately realized that can be my response when people ask me what it is like to paddle 100 miles on the Allagash Wilderness Waterway.

The Voice made me pause and feel Maine-tainer merge with the "AT". I ask myself, hmm, so that is what it is like to have the AT talk to me.

Topo Man made my imagination go wild, and his appearance with Compass was unexpected and appropriate. I could see a person tattooed from head to foot with the map of the AT, and yet this person was always losing his way on the AT.

If you want a book to tell you directions and points of interest on the AT, as most AT books do, then this book is not for you. If you want to "feel" this man's connection to the AT, and would enjoy a more poetic account of an AT thru-hike, then buy Dreaming the Appalachian Trail.

I felt so moved after reading Dreaming the Appalachian Trail I posted a five-star(*****)review on Amazon.com

Purchase *Dreaming the Appalachian Trail*
To buy **Dreaming...** ($10.00 72 pages) go to Amazon.com or
Xlibris Online Book Store

Brad's writings include special outdoor enthusiast columns
describing his personal exploits. You can read his outdoor pieces
by Googling keywords, "Brad Viles Maine".

Enthusiast passes on tips, stories, love of outdoors
In the January 16, 2010 issue of the Bangor Daily news, Brad
wrote a book review of **Outdoor Enthusiast** titled, Enthusiast
passes on tips, stories, love of outdoors. Click here to read it.

My Maine Connection
In the process of interviewing me for his BDN article, I recalled
my Maine adventures - after all, this review is for "Mainers".

Gosh, I am really connected! Not only was my Dad from Maine, I
have aunts and cousins throughout Maine, and we are doing a
genealogy search to verify that my great great grandmother was
indeed a Native American Indian.

Moreover, **Outdoor Enthusiast** describes seven of many paddling
treks in Maine including my three trips to the Allagash, the
Kenduskeag Stream Canoe Race (with my televised flip trying to
run Six-mile Falls), Kennebunk Fireman Triathlon, Kennebec
White Water Rafting, Maine Senior Games Cape Elizabeth
Triathlon, and the Androscoggin Trek to the Sea. My Maine club
memberships are the Appalachian Mountain Club and the Maine
Island Trail Association.

I trust my motivational presentation at the Naval Ship Yard in
Kittery, Maine encouraged sailors to enjoy Maine's outdoor
opportunities. Both **Outdoor Enthusiast: Never say, 'I wish I
had ...",** and **Outdoor Play Fun 4 4 Seasons** have *Places to Play
in Northern New England - the Maine Way.*

Be sure to never say, "I wish I had spent $10.00 to read,
Dreaming the Appalachian Trail

**Brad W. Viles, 63, died Jan. 22, 2012, in Millinocket.
He was born Oct. 4, 1948, in Portland, Maine.**

Video Reference Dreaming the Appalachian Trail
- Blog: Dreaming the Appalachian Trail
  http://outdooradventurers.blogspot.com/201
  0/01/dreaming-appalachian-trail.html

Places to Play in Northern New England

"Nothing preaches better than the act"
- Benjamin Franklin

*For all sad words of tongue or pen, the saddest of
all are these: "It might have been."*
- Whittier, Maud Muller

The choice of outdoor sports in northern New England is nearly
endless--ranging from hiking to biking to running to skiing to
snowshoeing, etc. There are literally thousands of mountains,
lakes and rivers here. With its four-season weather, an outdoor
enthusiast never runs out of a sport to "play".

The Internet is a major tool for locating outdoor sporting events,
organizations, instruction and outdoor blogs. Searching on
keywords such as, "Hiking in Vermont," "Cross country skiing in
New Hampshire", and "Paddling in Maine," reveals hundreds of
web sites. Enter "outdoor sports in northern New England" and
you will see hundreds of sites to choose from and a variety of
events in which to participate, learn, and never say, "I wish I
had...".

Discussions with other outdoor enthusiasts will reveal personal
sports of interest and places to visit and experience.

Outdoor enthusiasts with an interest in triathlons can go to
www.trifind.com, pick a state, and find a triathlon club, races, and
coaches.

Most organizations, such as the Appalachian Mountain Club
(AMC), Catamount Trail Organization, Peabody Mill
Environmental Center (PMEC), and Audubon Society have web
sites with email lists and e-newsletters which routinely announce
upcoming events.

Some organizations have diverse group activities. For example, the **Appalachian Mountain Club** (AMC) has an "Over 55 Club", a "Young Members Club", and "Singles Club. The **Peabody Mill Environmental Center** (PMEC) has everyday wooded trail hikes and snowshoeing, and monthly "fireside chats" where experienced outdoor enthusiasts share their knowledge through presentations and demonstrations. The **Catamount Trail Organization** schedules group skis. **The Granite State Wheelmen** and the **Green Mountain Bicycle Club** offer group rides and workshops.

The New Hampshire web site http://northeastmultisport.com/ offers a variety of triathlon oriented Clinics and Events for its members to improve performance as well as to encourage teammate camaraderie: bike time trials on summer evenings; winter fun runs for members to enjoy non-competitive group runs; transition clinics for tips and practice to minimize the time from swim to bike, and bike to run; and early morning open water group swims at local lakes.

Join organizations and clubs dedicated to encouraging and providing outdoor sports and recreation, so as to never have to say, **"I wish I had researched, investigated, and visited places to play in my own community".**

Inter-State Opportunities for Outdoor Play

Northern New England has many scenic, relaxing, and simply exciting inter-state outdoor opportunities for all seasons. Certainly waterways, forest trails and mountains have no sense of state boundaries. Here are five non-profit organizations offering unique places to play in northern New England.

The **Northern Forest Canoe Trail**, **Appalachian Trail**, **Androscoggin River**, **Great North Woods**, and **Maine Island Trail** will each be highlighted.

The Northern Forest Canoe Trail (NFCT)

http://www.northernforestcanoetrail.org/ links the waterways of New York, Vermont, Québec, New Hampshire and Maine.

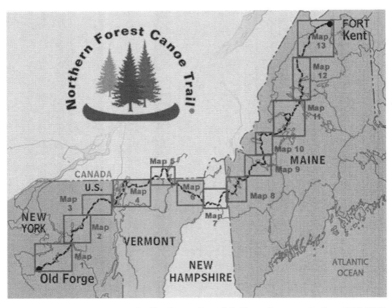

Figure 249 - Map defining the 13 Sections of the NFCT

The NFCT is a long-distance paddling trail connecting the major watersheds across the Adirondacks and Northern New England. The Trail links communities and wild places offering canoeists and kayakers a lifetime of paddling destinations within the 740-mile traverse across New York, Vermont, Quebec, New Hampshire, and Maine. The NFCT includes flat and whitewater paddling, poling, lining, and portaging (62 portages totaling 55 miles).

A visit to the NFCT can be a day-trip, an overnighter, weeks, or months. As hikers do sections of the Appalachian Trail, so do paddlers do the NFCT. You can put-in and take-out at any appropriate location. The NFCT organization is a great resource for your trip planning with web links and contact information.

Scheduled regional presentations by NFCT staff can be viewed on the NFCT web site. See the Planning link at the site for guidebooks and maps. http://bit.ly/Y3t48h

The sections to date of the NFCT that friends and I have paddled are:

- The Allagash Wilderness Waterway

- Lake Umbagog; Androscoggin River

- Lake Memphremagog

- Connecticut River

- Moose River and Attean Pond on the historic "Moose River Bow Trip"

- Umbazooksus Stream.

Posts on my blog for my section travels on the NFCT are:

- Paddling the Northern Forest Canoe Trail Section 2: Long Lake to Village of Saranac Lake http://outdooradventurers.blogspot.com/2014/06/paddling-northern-forest-canoe-trail.html

- Paddling the Northern Forest Canoe Trail Section 6: The Clyde River - Island Pond to Pensioner Pond http://outdooradventurers.blogspot.com/2013/06/paddling-northern-forest-canoe-trail.html

- Four Days in Northern New Hampshire with Family and Friends Hiking, Paddling, Tenting and Moose Sighting. http://outdooradventurers.blogspot.com/2012/07/four-days-in-new-hampshire-of-family.html

- Exploring Lake Umbagog – a Gem in the Great North Woods http://outdooradventurers.blogspot.com/2010/09/exploring-lake-umbagog-gem-in-great.html

- Paddling the Allagash Wilderness Waterway http://outdooradventurers.blogspot.com/2009/07/paddling-allagash-wilderness-waterway.html

Appalachian Trail
The AT in northern New England passes through Vermont and New Hampshire and has its northern terminus at the summit of Mt Katahdin in Maine.

Figure 250 - Map of Appalachian Trail from Maine to Georgia

I recommend two references to get started with understanding the AT:

1) **The Appalachian Trail Conservancy**
   (http://www.appalachiantrail.org/)
2) **The Appalachian Mountain Club** (AMC)
   (http://www.outdoors.org/)

The Appalachian Trail Conservancy

(http://www.appalachiantrail.org/) preserves and manages the Appalachian Trail – ensuring that its vast natural beauty and priceless cultural heritage can be shared and enjoyed today, tomorrow, and for centuries to come.

The Appalachian Mountain Club (AMC)

(http://www.outdoors.org/) promotes the protection, enjoyment, and understanding of the mountains, forests, waters, and trails of the Appalachian region.

Paddling with the AMC

The New Hampshire Appalachian Mountain Club Paddlers web site (http://www.nhamcpaddlers.org/) is an excellent resource for places to paddle in New Hampshire. The Paddlers welcome beginners, intermediate and experienced paddlers, 16 and older, who are interested in paddling safely while having a great time.

The Paddlers site has a free e-mail sign up for monthly notices of Paddler happenings. The emails include weekend and weekday trips, items for sale by members, such as canoes, kayaks, racks, and other paddling equipment and Paddler events.

The Paddlers web site encourages you to join the Appalachian Mountain Club (http://www.outdoors.org).

The NH AMC Paddlers web site "Places to Paddle" link (http://www.nhamcpaddlers.org/m_content/places.htm) has directions and descriptions to over twenty lake, river and marsh paddling trips, all in New Hampshire. Other links include, "Upcoming Trips" where you can join others for scheduled trips.

The NH AMC Paddlers have canoe and kayak paddles weekday evenings throughout the summer.

Four of my Blog posts on the AT:
- **Dreaming the Appalachian Trail**
  http://outdooradventurers.blogspot.com/2010/01/dreaming-appalachian-trail.html
- **Springer Mountain, Georgia - Southern Terminus of the Appalachian Trail**
  http://outdooradventurers.blogspot.com/2009/11/springer-mountain-georgia-southern.html
- **A Mid-week Trek to Tuckerman Ravine**
  http://outdooradventurers.blogspot.com/2009/04/fantastic-mid-week-trek-to-tuckerman.html
- **Hiking Mount Chocorua - White Mountain National Forest**
  http://outdooradventurers.blogspot.com/2011/08/hiking-mount-chocorua-white-mountain.html

Androscoggin River

The Androscoggin River is a major river in northern New England. The Androscoggin headwaters are in Errol, New Hampshire, where the Magalloway River joins the outlet of Umbagog Lake. It is 178 miles long and joins the Kennebec River at Merrymeeting Bay in Maine before its water empties into the Gulf of Maine on the Atlantic Ocean. Its drainage basin is 3,530 square miles (9,100 km2) in area.

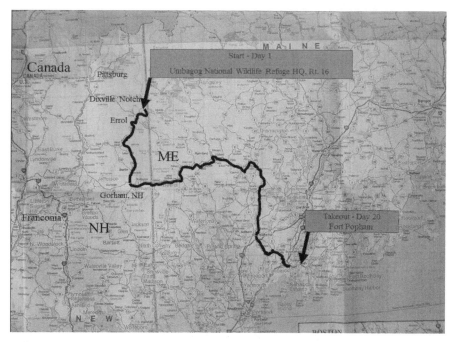

Figure 251 - Map - The Androscoggin River Source to the Sea

The Androscoggin River Water Shed Council
http://arwc.camp7.org/ offers protection, history and paddling
groups on the Androscoggin River. The ARWC sponsors the
Source to the Sea Trek http://arwc.camp7.org/trek.

Outdoor Steve has paddled twelve sections of this Trek and you
can find numerous descriptions of his fabulous paddle at
http://www.outdoorsteve.com/. For articles and other stories such
as **Androscoggin River Source to the Sea Canoe and Kayak
Trek**
visithttp://www.outdoorsteve.com/_pdffiles/8_20Mar05_Andro
scogginRiverSourcetotheSea_NewsSentinel.pdf.

Interestingly, 19 miles of the Androscoggin River headwaters are
also part of the Northern Forest Canoe Trail (NFCT)!

Great North Woods
Northern New Hampshire, also known as the Great North Woods
Region, is the official state tourist region located in Coos County.

This area includes Northern New Hampshire, bordering Northeast Kingdom Vermont, and unincorporated townships in the northern and northwestern part of Maine

Ten Things to do in the Great North Woods of New Hampshire
(http://www.newhampshire.com/article/99999999/NEWHAMP
SHIRE05/110429465

Great North Woods Online
(http://greatnorthwoodsonline.com/)

Enjoy the Great North Woods
http://www.outdoorsteve.com/_pdffiles/23_21Jun08_Great_No
rth_Woods_NewHampshire.com.pdf

A Hike to Table Rock, Dixville, New Hampshire
http://outdooradventurers.blogspot.com/2010/07/hike-to-table-
rock-dixville-new.html

Maine Island Trail (MIT)
http://www.mita.org/

The MIT begins at Maine's coastal border with New Hampshire and ends in Machias, Maine, with an additional collection of two islands in Passamaquoddy Bay and the New Brunswick region of Canada.

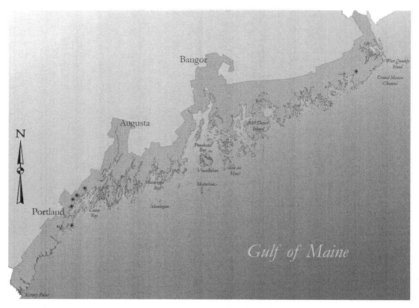

Figure 252 - Overview of Maine Island Trail

The Maine Island Trail is a 375-mile-long waterway along the coast of <u>Maine</u> that connects approximately 200 islands and mainland sites available for day visits or overnight camping. The trail is maintained by the <u>Maine Island Trail Association (MITA)</u>.

Through partnerships with the State of Maine, as well as land trusts, non-profit organizations, and generous private property owners, MITA ensures access to these sites for visitors in kayaks, sailboats, motorboats, and other watercraft. In exchange for access, MITA members agree to visitation guidelines set by the island owners and provide a wide range of stewardship services including island monitoring and management by trained volunteers with organized regional island cleanups each year.

FAQ on Site Reservations

The only sites (public or private) on the **Maine Island Trail** that take reservations are Warren Island, Swan Island (Kennebec), Cobscook Bay State Park, and Butter and Burnt Islands. All others are first-come first-served (FCFS). Details are in the member Trail Guide. The MITA advises people to have a backup in mind and arrive with time to spare. However, the fact is that except for peak weekends on smaller most favored islands, people typically do not report difficulties. There are a lot of islands to go around!

See the **Outdoor Enthusiast** blog post on Steve's Maine Island Trail trek.

- **Blog: Places to Play in Northern New England**
  http://outdooradventurers.blogspot.com/2013/02/places-to-play-in-northern-new-england.html
- **Blog: Sea Kayaking and Camping on the Maine Island Trail**
  http://outdooradventurers.blogspot.com/2010/08/sea-kayaking-and-camping-on-maine.html

New Hampshire

Live Free or Die

New Hampshire – Your Own Backyard

✓ New Hampshire AMC Paddlers (www.nhamcpaddlers.org)
✓ Appalachian Mountain Club (www. outdoors.org)
✓ Local Hikes (www.localhikes.com)
✓ The Slackpacker (www.slackpacker.com)
✓ Granite State Wheelmen (www.granitestatewheelmen.org)
✓ New Hampshire State Parks (www.nhstateparks.com)
✓ Outdoor Steve (www.outdoorsteve.com)
✓ Granite State Senior Games (50+)(www.nhseniorgames.org)

Figure 253 - Places to Play in New Hampshire

Below is but a small sample of paddling opportunities in southern New Hampshire.

- Veterans Park on Naticook Lake in Merrimack NH
  http://bluetoad.com/display_article.php?id=1127713

- Nashua River. A good put-in behind Stellos Stadium.

- Great Turkey Pond, west of Concord NH.

- Lake Massabesic, East of Manchester NH in Auburn. Many put-ins. Try the Auburn Town Beach.

- Hopkinton Lake west of Concord NH. Exit 5 Rte 89 west of Concord NH

- Hoit Road Marsh north of Concord NH

- Glen Lake in Goffstown, NH

- Dubes Pond, in Hooksett, NH. GPS has it at 270 Whitehall Road, Hooksett, NH

- McDaniel's Marsh. Exit 13 from I89 to East Grantham. Route 114 to West Springfield. North on George's Hill Road. At intersection of Bog Road and Georges Hill Road. The Marsh put-in is directly across from Bog Road.

- Merrimack River. Many put-ins and take-outs. One put-in is the boat ramp behind Franklin High School. Paddle 10.5 miles to Boscawen ball fields takes about 4-5 hrs.

Hiking Year Round

- o **Welch-Dickey Mountain Trail**
  A unique scenic loop over and around the summits of two mountains. Great view of Mad River in Waterville Valley. A 4.5-mile scenic loop. In wet weather the bare rock may be slippery, so this is definitely a summer hike. Located I-93 via Exit 28.
  http://tiny.cc/9yoruw

Figure 254 - Welch-Dickey Trail

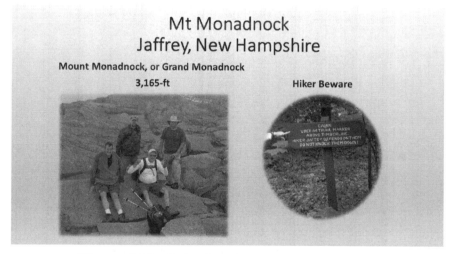

Figure 255 - Relaxing Atop Mt Monadnock

- o   Mount Monadnock Southwestern, NH
      3,165-ft. Mt. 40 miles of maintained foot trails. 100-mile
      views into all six New England states. Second most
      frequently climbed mountain in the world, after Mount Fuji
      in Japan. http://tiny.cc/xr9m5x

- o   **Mount Willard Trail**, White Mountains, NH
      The Mount Willard Trail leads from the AMC Crawford

Notch Visitor Center to scenic ledges overlooking Crawford Notch. Two hour round trip hike. Just fine for a family day hike. http://tiny.cc/kqoruw

- **Cohos Trail**
  The Cohos Trail is New England's newest long-distance hiking route, extending 162 miles through the woods and mountains of northern New Hampshire. Most likely, you will have a day of absolute solitude. http://www.cohostrail.org/

- **Mount Kearsarge**
  Directions: Wilmot and Warner, New Hampshire. From Route 89 take Route 11. 2,937 foot summit, length: 2.2 miles http://tiny.cc/naan5x.

Figure 256 - The Peak of Mt Kearsarge

Local References with Nearby City Trails & Maps

- Where best to look for "places to play" than in your own backyard. I entered keywords, "Bedford New Hampshire hiking trails" into my browser, and saw http://www.traillink.com/city/bedford-nh-trails.aspx. The site easily identified:

  o Bedford Biking Trails

  o Bedford Running Trails

  o Bedford Walking Trails

  o Nearby City Trails & Maps

- Entering keywords, "Sunapee New Hampshire hiking Trails" I found: http://www.lakesunapeenh.org/discover/hiking-lake-sunapee-region/. This reference includes New London, NH and a list of organizations and town conservation commissions which offer trail maps that include hiking opportunities within the Mt. Kearsarge/Lake Sunapee region:

Maine

Maine – Your Own Backyard

✓Maine Island Trail (www.mita.org)
✓Maine Outdoors (www.maineoutdoors.com)
✓Local Hikes (www.localhikes.com)
✓The Slackpacker (www.slackpacker.com)
✓The Loonsnest (www.loonsnest.biz)
✓Outdoor Steve (www.outdoorsteve.com)
✓Maine Senior Games (50+) (www.mainesrgames.org)
✓Granite State Senior Games (50+)(www.nhseniorgames.org)

Figure 257 - Places to Play in Maine

Hiking

- **Hiking in Maine** is a popular reference for hiking trails. Maine has a variety of hiking options available. Trails can be above tree line, trails meander through cool pine forests, and trails run along Maine's rugged coast. http://www.maineoutdoors.com/hiking/hike_info_trails. shtml

- **Slackpacker.com** provides access to informative Maine hiking websites. Hikers post comments on their personal hiking experiences, thus making research easier to get "an up front and personal" sense of the trails difficulties. http://www.slackpacker.com

- **The Local Hikes** provides information on local hiking opportunities in all areas of the United States. You can find a preferred trail by selecting your metro area, browse the available hikes, or by using the search feature to find the trails closest to your home or office. The hikes reviewed on this site are contributed by volunteer hikers. http://www.localhikes.com

Canoeing and Kayaking

- **The Loon's Nest** specializes in wilderness river canoe trips. This site specializes in all forms of outdoor wilderness recreation and is a wealth of information about animals; (hear the four major loon calls); has a fantastic photo gallery of outstanding outdoor pictures taken in all seasons from summer canoeing, sailing, and hiking to winter xc skiing and snowshoeing; as well as many beautiful photographs of Maine's wildlife caught in their natural habitat. http://www.loonsnest.biz

The Maine Island Trail
http://www.mita.org

See the narrative earlier in this section for Maine Island Trail with over 200 islands to "play" on.

Northern Forest Canoe Trail
http://www.northernforestcanoetrail.org/

The NFCT has over 345 miles traversing some of the most scenic, remote, and rugged landscapes that Maine has to offer.

Vermont

Freedom and Unity

Vermont – Your Own Backyard

✓ Vermont Living (www.vtliving.com)
✓ Green Mountain Club(www.greenmountainclub.org)
✓ Local Hikes (www.localhikes.com)
✓ The Slackpacker (www.slackpacker.com)
✓ Catamount Trail(www.catamounttrail.org)
✓ Frozen Bullet(www.frozenbullet.com)
✓ Vermont Senior Games(50+)
(www.seniorgames.org/stategames.htm)

Figure 258 - Places to Play in Vermont

Hiking

- **Vermont Living** and **Trails.com** web sites have trails and backpacking areas
  http://www.vtliving.com/hiking/
  http://www.trails.com/toptrails.aspx?area=10012

- The **Long Trail** was built by the **Green Mountain Club** between 1910 and 1930. The Long Trail is the oldest long-distance trail in the United States. The Long Trail follows the main ridge of the Green Mountains from the Massachusetts-Vermont line to the Canadian border as it crosses Vermont's highest peaks.
  http://www.greenmountainclub.org/

Canoeing and Kayaking

- **Vermont Living** is a good site to locate places in VT for canoeing and kayaking. Some of Vermont's most notable canoeing and kayaking waterways include the Connecticut River that serves as the border between VT and NH, the Batten Kill in southeastern VT, the Lamoille which crosses Vermont's northern region, the Missisquoi in the northwest corner, and the Winooski and White Rivers in north central Vermont http://www.vtliving.com/canoeing/index.shtml.

- **Northern Forest Canoe Trail** has over 170 miles in Vermont and Quebec http://www.northernforestcanoetrail.org/

- **Outdoor Enthusiast: Never say, "I wish I had…":** both the 2009 and 2014 hardcopies and the updated 2014 e-book have more Vermont "places to play".

XC Skiing

- **The Catamount Trail (CAT)**

  The CAT traverses approximately 130 miles of public land including the Green Mountain National Forest, Vermont state land, and town-owned parcels. It is divided into 31 sections. The CAT is appropriate for a broad range of skiing and snowshoeing abilities.
  http://www.catamounttrail.org

  Biathlon
  - The United States Biathlon site is a good reference to biathlon events and places for instruction and training.
    http://www.teamusa.org/US-Biathlon.aspx

  - Go to **How Stuff Works** to learn more about the rules and basics of the biathlon.
    http://adventure.howstuffworks.com/outdoor-activities/snow-sports/biathlon.htm

Senior Games

Encouragement of healthy lifestyles certainly includes outdoor activities for senior athletes. **The National Senior Games Association (NSGA)** is a not-for-profit member of the United States Olympic Committee dedicated to motivating senior men and women to lead a healthy lifestyle through senior athletics.

NSGA is an umbrella for state organizations across the United States that host State Senior Games or Senior Olympics. States have both winter and summer athletic games for female and male athletes over 50 years young. Games may include triathlons, cycling, race walking, track and field events, swimming, road races, pistol shooting, archery, and golf. Some states do paddling, downhill skiing, and cross-country skiing.

New Hampshire, Maine and Vermont are very active both within their states and in national competitions.

- o **National Senor Games Association**
  http://www.nsga.com/
- o **Granite State Senior Games**
  http://www.nhseniorgames.org/
- o **Maine Senior Games**
  http://www.smaaa.org/maine_senior_games.php
- o **Vermont Senior Games**
  http://www.vermontseniorgames.org/

So What Do You Do Now?

This Northern New England section is but the tip of the iceberg to locate areas of opportunity, clubs, organizations and fellow outdoor enthusiasts. Local activities are often in our own backyards, and are located by looking in newspaper sections for Outdoor Activities or simply by Internet searching for events in your city or town.

Use Google key words (such as orienteering, biathlon, bicycle clubs, snowshoe, etc) to search for locations and sports of interest near you.

Conditioning

The beginning of this book offers **How to be an Outdoor Enthusiast.** It describes a process of physical fitness and how it directly relates to mental preparation and health. Knowing one is not in shape makes it very easy to rationalize postponing an adventure. Moreover, without proper conditioning, we make our companions and ourselves susceptible to injury and failure. Physical fitness complements mental fitness.

The Commitment

A major part of adventure commitment is preparation. The weeks and months before an event are critical. This starts with a mental walk-through of the event itself and working backwards to create a check-off list of things to do and when they are to be done. Do you need campsite reservations? Must you register for the event?

Registration is part of the commitment. When there is a delay in registration, the commitment is not there. A registration commitment can include hotel, campsite or airline reservations.

There must be a plan to reach the required level of physical conditioning. Physical conditioning for a triathlon is much different from white water rafting. Most adventures require stamina, endurance, and quick recovery from cardio exertion. A daily running routine - four to five days a week - provides a baseline conditioning level from which specific conditioning exercises, such as upper body weight training, can support an adventure, such as kayaking and canoeing.

We need to know the extremes of weather we may encounter and plan accordingly. The expected weather conditions may mean gathering specific weather-related clothing, food and medical supplies.

Other preparations, such as for hiking, may include developing skills for map and compass reading. If we work backward from the event, this should provide us a checklist upon which to plan our preparations (i.e. scheduling our time, equipment needs, and training). If you are going winter camping, you might practice by sleeping in your backyard to learn what you need for comfort. It is far better to know your sleeping bag does not support cold weather camping when you are in your own backyard rather than to discover this when you are in the middle of the mountains miles away from your car!

Let's continue to play. To enjoy play, one must be physically ready. Hence, exercise is a key enabler of "play." Knowing I have tried, for me, is as important as winning. Regardless of success or failure, my participation provides a never-ending sense of achievement. To me, participation at any level is more rewarding than observation of the highest level.

We need to commit to never say, "I wish I had". Once we have done that - and this could be a financial commitment such as a membership in an outdoor organization such as the YMCA outdoor club or the Appalachian Mountain Club. Then we need to commit to a training program.

We also must recognize it is OK to finish 485th out of 501 entered in a race. It is also OK to finish last! After all, someone has to, why not me! We need to realize that we do not need to go to the other side of the world to achieve a dream. If we simply look around we can see roads for running, lakes for paddling, and woods and mountains for hiking. Even our own backyards can supply the opportunity for the "snow-cave" you might want to build.

A nice thing about being an outdoor enthusiast is that most activities cost only our time. A small investment in a canoe, running shoes, bicycle, or cross-country skis will be enough to give us a lifetime of adventure. We often need to look no further than magazines and newspapers to see these opportunities.

If I have shared my story appropriately, I have both encouraged and supported your enthusiasm for a daily outdoors commitment, made you crave your own "beginnings", and have given insights into new outdoor activities and places to go.

I will thus have achieved my goal of helping others become an "Outdoor Enthusiast" and forever make "Outdoor Play" a component of their daily life.

Never say, "I wish I could find an outdoor activity close to my home."

The Beginning

- *In the long run one hits only what they aim at. Therefore, though they should fail immediately, they had better aim at something high.*– Henry David Thoreau, Walden
- *Give yourself permission to dream - Randy Pausch*
- *The journey of a thousand miles begins with one step. - Miryamoto Musashi*

Introduction

This last section of the book is my beginning. I put it here to not take away from the reader's self-motivation. I add it to further encourage individuals and families to make the outdoors a part of their daily lives. And here is my start.

Have you ever thought about sleeping overnight in a snow cave, built by yourself, in the middle of the wilderness? How about running a marathon? What about canoeing through white water, visiting a Shaker museum, or attending a lecture on alternative medicine therapies?

Some folks call these outdoor experiences 'play'. If play is defined as the choice made to take a course of action based on the rewards of participation, and getting a perspective that can only come from 'doing', outdoor adventures are indeed play. Many folks, both adults and children, do not play enough. Play is personal and winning is of no importance. Outdoor play should be a daily component of life.

"I wish I had..." is an expression people often mutter as they rationalize their regret for not having done something. Is it better to have tried and failed than never to have tried at all? Absolutely! Certainly, physical limitations may relate to achievement, but sometimes we erect personal barriers of embarrassment, reluctance, and other self-administrated hurdles.

Try an outdoor trek. Take a chance and peek into a side of outdoor life observed by only the few that do take the chance. How do you describe how beautiful Allagash Falls is at dawn? You can view a thousand pictures, but until you exit your tent at first light, you will never truly know what it is like to experience the sun popping into the sky.

The Opportunity: The Torn Achilles Tendon

Any enthusiast needs to start somewhere. My outdoor emergence began while in an injured state: I had been a couch potato absorbed with the pressures and problems of work, and felt no commitment to outdoor activities other than mowing the lawn. Taking time to 'smell the roses' was not a scheduled event, and surely visiting museums was not a part of my lifestyle.

Maybe the outdoor enthusiasm all started with the "good fortune" of tearing my Achilles tendon. Coincidentally, this injury came two years after I had completed my Masters dissertation in Management Engineering with a thesis entitled, The Achilles Tendon as an Indication of Thyroid Function. Years later the anatomy studies required to understand the function of the Achilles tendon helped me to accept my injury.

My injury came as I was playing basketball in a pick-up game. I had positioned myself for a clear outside shot and was in the process of shooting the ball. Suddenly I felt as if someone had hit me in the back of my ankle. I dropped to the floor, and turned around expecting to see who had taken my legs out from under me. Nobody was there. The damage was done – my Achilles tendon had ruptured.

The healing process progressed erratically. A noticeable indentation appeared where the tear had taken place. The medical opinion was that surgical treatment would not necessarily help. Medical professionals told me there was a fifty - fifty chance that the tendon would tear again. I was determined to prove them wrong.

The First Mile

One day, about a year after my injury, I decided to do something about my twenty-five pound weight gain, a perpetual "tired feeling", and general lack of exercise. I went down to my cellar and rummaged through old boxes of shoes. I found my ten-year-old ankle-high Army combat boots and reminisced to myself about boot camp and its daily mandate to hit the road running.

Figure 259 - The Army Combat Boots

The boots were intact, though the leather was a bit stiff and definitely needed a softener. I ignored the tautness, and proceeded to lace them tight in the hopes of ensuring protection for my "healed" Achilles tendon. Now was the time to determine if exercise would free me from my couch.

I went outside and ran - maybe limped is a better word - a distance of two telephone poles. Even though I was breathing heavily and perspiring profusely, it felt good, despite the sensitivity of a now sore tendon.

The next evening, I climbed back into my combat boots. This time with a determination to exceed the previous day's run of two telephone poles. I lumbered, limped, and puffed to achieve the distance of three telephone poles. My quest had begun.

Figure 260 - Walk-Run Between Two Telephone Poles

Daily, after work, I continued extending my distances one pole at a time. My Achilles tendon threat to tear again concerned me, but I fervently decided against returning to inactivity.

Initially, my running goals were measured in terms of those ever-present telephone poles. However, after two weeks, I abandoned this strategy, and I reset my goals to reach the end of my street without stopping - about a third of a mile. By the end of the third week, not only had I achieved my objective, but I also turned around and began running back home.

I now had a dream that one day - maybe, just maybe - I could jog around my neighborhood block. I measured the distance with my car and determined the loop was exactly a mile. Each evening I came closer to completing the neighborhood loop, but exhaustion resulted in walking before I died. Five weeks had elapsed since my emergence from the couch. Each day at work, I would picture myself accomplishing the mile. Every evening I would start, determined to run the one-mile route, only to end up walking.

During week six, I had a feeling that this was to be my time, my day. I saw my house in the distance, and was having no difficulty breathing. I had no thoughts about my Achilles, and until this moment, I was simply concentrating on an issue at work. I suddenly realized I was less than four telephone poles from my quest. With painful joy shared with no one but myself, in what seemed to be mere seconds, my goal was now history. Sucking air with sheer exhaustion, I stumbled into my backyard overjoyed with the thrill of victory.

I ran this one-mile loop - usually six days a week - for nearly two years with no thought of extending my distance. Certainly, other outdoor challenges, such as biking, canoeing, hiking and kayaking, were not even a consideration.

One day I read in the local newspaper about a seven-mile running race. The race was four weeks away. I dared to think that perhaps I could finish this distance. I began extending my daily run, and in one week I was able to do my one-mile loop twice! I had doubled my distance in only one week. I set my next goal at four miles and accomplished it within two weeks. It was now time for me to assess myself against other athletes. I submitted my entry form.

The appropriately named Freedom Trail race was a seven-miler at the University of Massachusetts campus at Dartmouth. My pre-race jitters were compounded by second-guessing myself as to whether I should even be here. I had never participated in any type of official running race before, and I had visions of being elbowed and trampled by a pack of passionate runners.

I overcame this distress by positioning myself at the back of the mass of lightly clad runners who were stretching, jumping up and down, and obviously trying to relieve their nerves while waiting for the start of the race.

I had anticipated all participants to be thin, athletic, and young. Instead, I encountered all types, men and women, young and old, and people in various degrees of physical shape - thin, fat, short, tall, and pudgy. Naively, I thought that I surely would finish in front of the older and overweight athletes.

I got a quick education when the official fired the starter's gun. After a few hundred feet, not only was I holding up the rear, I was yards behind the last runner. I began to have thoughts of not finishing, and worse, becoming lost as the runners in front of me continued to get further ahead. At the second mile marker, a few runners were still in sight, and I resigned myself simply to completing the race.

At the five-mile marker, I was running side by side with a young woman who appeared to be in her late twenties. We were the last two racers. I was sure she had slowed down to let me catch up, because I knew I was in no condition to speed up. We talked about our jobs and our families - anything to help forget the pain we were both experiencing.

With about a mile to go to the finish line, she suggested we pick up our speed. Unfortunately, I was already at my maximum speed. Off she went, with my blessings, and I was the last runner to cross the finish line. To top things off, there were only two people at the finish line - my wonderful mother and the timer. My mother would not let the timer leave until I had finished!

The immediate aftermath of this seven-mile "triumph" was that I could not sit down! Every time I tried to bend my legs and lower myself to the ground, my hamstrings would begin to cramp.

Indeed, I was a "winner", but I now had to pay the price of my personal best distance.

The outcome of this story was that I had run seven miles! Little did I know at the time this experience would be the beginning of a lifetime enjoyment of outdoor challenges.

Certainly, a benefit of physical conditioning was my weight loss of nearly forty pounds. I felt different both physically and mentally. The seat of my pants was floppy and my face lost its fullness. Friends began to ask if I was "sick". I had to buy new suits. It felt great being asked all these personal questions!

A Family Revelation

My outdoor enthusiasm carried forth to my family as we began to participate together in outdoor fun and exercise. My wife and I regularly walk and run together. A summer night can find us kayaking or canoeing on the lakes of New Hampshire.

My two sons and my grandchildren are essential components to my daily outdoor life. As a family, our activities include hiking, canoeing, kayaking, running, and morning and evening moose sightings.

Let me relate a father-son-revelation that occurred while hiking with my son Timothy when he was a teenager. Hiking provides an opportunity to share experiences on an adult level and leave behind the typical parent/child relationship of the home environment. Hiking in the mountains requires reliance upon your partner that breaks down parent/child barriers that develop from the routine of daily life. At home, the parent sets an example and provides the child with an opportunity to learn. This pattern must be adjusted in the wilderness.

Tim and I lumbered along the Appalachian Trail planning to spend the night at the Mizpah Spring hut, one of the eight White Mountain huts maintained by the New Hampshire Chapter of the Appalachian Mountain Club. Just as we reached the peak of Mt.

Franklin, the weather quickly changed and it began to rain. The rain became heavy, the sky grew darker, and suddenly we were engulfed in a torrent of rain. Driving rain pelted us, and thunder and lightning roared and crackled all around. It was only three o'clock in the afternoon and yet it was nearly pitch dark. It was a strange and awesome sensation. The top of Mt Franklin is entirely ledge and rock, and we knew immediately we were in a dangerous position - on top of a mountain and without shelter. It was a bizarre and scary feeling as we stood there in our rain suits, rain pouring off our faces and our features illuminated sporadically by flashes of light.

An unbelievable sensation of excitement and strength came over me. I felt I united with the earth and the elements and had all their power at my command. At the same time, I feared that this angry and violent deluge would overcome us, and we might not survive this encounter. I suddenly knew before Tim or I died - and it could have happened at any moment - I wanted Tim to know how much a part of me he was. I had an unbelievable urge to hug Tim, kiss him, and tell him how much I loved and admired him - and so I did! It was a moment I still remember today - hugging my teenage son with all my strength and telling him how much he meant to me.

Meanwhile thunder crackled and lightening illuminated the darkness, filling the surrounding countryside with shadows and ghostly sensations. We were in the middle of an enormous storm, terrifying, yet beautiful at the same time.

Tim responded to my hug and kiss with the same embracing closeness and finality that I did. I could feel his strength and our oneness as he embraced me for what could be the last time.

Then, just as suddenly as the storm had come, it was gone. The sun came out as if to say, "Together you have seen the light and felt your courage and unity." We were wet and shivering, but thankfully we were without injury. We continued our journey.

Tim had avoided my invitations to learn in the past - that is what it seemed to me. Our stay at Mizpah Spring showed I was wrong.

The volunteer naturalist at the hut led an evening tour to learn about the birds, animals, shrubs and trees native to this high altitude habitat. With obvious interest, Tim asked many questions of the naturalist.

A sunrise tour for a different aspect of the habitat was scheduled. Given the previous day's tiring adventures, I never expected to see Tim. We went to bed that night, exhausted.

At 4:45 AM, my watch alarm went off and I quietly whispered to Tim I was getting up for the tour. I left the bunkroom pleased at Tim's delight with the previous evening. To my surprise and much pleasure, who should appear at the morning walk-about but Tim!

Tim and I experienced a bonding on that hike we still discuss today. We depended on each other in a death-defying situation. I saw that he is caring, self-reliant, and levelheaded under pressure. He has a thirst to learn. I have come to recognize these qualities and more as we have shared the joys, challenges and revelations provided by hiking trips along the Appalachian Trail and many other "Outdoor Play" adventures.

If the facts be known, the awakening and growth in maturity was solely mine.

From the Outdoors to Intellectual Pursuits

Interestingly, this curiosity to experience new and different outdoor activities began to carry over to intellectual inquisitiveness and my mantra, "Never say, I wish I had...", I began to visit museums, simply to gain awareness of something new. I became obsessed with the opportunity to learn the unique and interesting worlds of others. Now I attend lectures with a craving to hear a speaker's insights, and to listen to his or her passion and enthusiasm. Certainly, this curiosity includes presentations on all facets of the outdoors found by simply looking through the local newspapers. Animal tracks, identifying trees, learning about turkeys, Mount Everest climbers, and seafaring presentations are all there, usually for free or a minimal fee.

So, What Do You Do Now?

If tearing my tendon made me recognize the limits of my knowledge and appreciation, the pain and struggle of recuperation was worth it.

This book shares short stories of outdoors and wilderness knowledge gained through personal involvement. It can be a guidebook of places and events to play. It is not a traditional how-to, or you-should kind of book, but life stories for individuals and families to motivate them to make the outdoors a daily part of life.

These stories are meant to stimulate the reader to enjoy the outdoor world and the people around them. The message is, "It is okay to listen to your inner calling." You will never regret that you did not experience the renewal and fulfillment venturing into the outdoors may provide. Simply being in an audience as others perform and share their views cannot satisfy an eager human being. The motivation is to "get off the couch," and not let others dictate what you know or do.

I do not want to pretend I am a philosopher of what life is about, or a preacher of outdoor activities, nor a non-conformist in life. Henry David Thoreau appears to express my approach to outdoor living. In Walden he said, "I went to the woods because I wished to live deliberately, to front only the essential facts of life, and to see if I could not learn what it had to teach, and not, when I came to die, discover that I had not lived. I wanted to live deep and suck out all the marrow of life..."

My Achilles tendon has never completely regenerated to its former strength. I sometimes have a noticeable limp at the end of a long day on my feet, but the limp has no pain and does not hinder any of my outdoor activities.

I mention my past injury because some people use self-imposed physical and mental barriers, and say, "I wish I could do physical exercise and outdoor adventures similar to yours, but I tore my Achilles tendon" (or whatever physical ailment they have). Other "wish I could" reasons I hear are, "I am too old", "I am way out of shape," and "I do not know where to start." Hmm, guess they did not read the first section in this book, **How to be an Outdoor Enthusiast.**

Be aware - outdoor enthusiasm includes family revelations. As I learned more about myself when hiking with Timothy and Shaun, so did I see my sons become mature and responsible adults. My sons and I have done numerous canoeing and kayaking trips and have sat beside campfires talking about life, ambitions, and family issues.

My wife Cathy and I regularly walk, hike, camp and paddle together. Most important are the conversations we have on our family, finances, and other life issues.

Never say, "I wish I had made the outdoors a part of my daily life."

Figure 261 - "Everyone must believe in something. I believe I'll go outdoors with my family." – S. Priest

Table of Figures

Books by Stephen L. Priest

- **Outdoor Play "Fun 4 4 Seasons" Volume I**
  Hard Copy
  https://www.createspace.com/4177334

  ISBN **978-0-985-03840-3**

- **Outdoor Play "Fun 4 4 Seasons" Volume I**
  Hard Copy **Special Edition Full Color**
  https://www.createspace.com/3745716

  ISBN **978-0-615-22504-3**

- **Outdoor Play "Fun 4 4 Seasons" Volume I**
  Amazon.com Kindle e-book
  http://www.amazon.com/dp/B00C2G20HQ

  ISBN **978-0-9850384-1-0**

- **Outdoor Enthusiast: Never say, "I wish I had ..."**
  Hardcopy
  https://www.createspace.com/3356777

  ISBN 1440438404

- **Outdoor Enthusiast: Never say, "I wish I had..."**
  Amazon.com Kindle e-book
  http://tiny.cc/d2c0t

  ISBN 9780615225050

- **Outdoor Enthusiast: Never say I wish I had..."**
  Barnes & Noble Nook e-book
  BN ID: 2940012341037
  http://tiny.cc/85ygs

  ISBN 9780615225050

- **Outdoor Enthusiast: Never say, "I wish I had…"**
  Amazon.com Hard Copy
  http://tiny.cc/lli3tw

   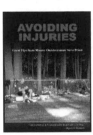

ISBN 1301078331

- **Avoiding Injuries: Great Tips From Master Outdoorsman Steve Priest**
  Create Space Hard Copy
  https://www.createspace.com/3356784

ISBN 9781440438455

Community Television Outdoor Documentaries by OutdoorSteve

Steve's below **Community Television Outdoor Documentaries** are available for community and non-profit organizations by **Bedford Community Television (BCTV)** at **603-472-8288** and http://www.bedfordtv.com/:

√ **ROWING through the eyes of a beginner** http://tiny.cc/c9ow6x

√ **Winter in New Hampshire is More Than Downhill Skiing** http://tiny.cc/t9ow6x

√ **Knife Edge Trail to Baxter Peak, Maine** http://tiny.cc/oapw6x

√ **Ice Boating in New Hampshire** http://tiny.cc/zapw6x

√ **Robert Frost's Apple Picking Time in New Hampshire** http://tiny.cc/0bpw6x

√ **Ocean Kayaking in the Deer Isle Region of the Maine Coast – Stonington to Isle au Haut** http://tiny.cc/6cpw6x

√ **Northern Forest Canoe Trail, Section 2, New York** http://tiny.cc/fdpw6x

√ **Northern Forest Canoe Trail, Section 6 Clyde River, Vermont** http://tiny.cc/4dpw6x

√ **Making an Ottertail Paddle** http://tiny.cc/pepw6x

√ Four Days in Northern New Hampshire Paddling and Moose Sighting **http://tiny.cc/kfpw6x**

√ **Goffstown Pumpkin Weigh-in and Regatta** http://tiny.cc/jgpw6x

√ **Re-using Outdoor Hand warmers** http://tiny.cc/8apw6x

Online access to the documentaries can be found at: http://www.OutdoorSteve.com and **http://outdooradventurers.blogspot.com/**

"Everyone must believe in something. I believe I'll go outdoors with my family and friends." – S. Priest

Notes

Outdoor Play "Fun 4 4 Seasons" Volume II